*The Sound of Undoing*

AMERICAN LIVES
*Series editor*: Tobias Wolff

# The

# Sound

# of

# Undoing

A Memoir in Essays

PAIGE TOWERS

University of Nebraska Press *Lincoln*

The University of Nebraska Press is part of a land-grant institution with campuses and programs on the past, present, and future homelands of the Pawnee, Ponca, Otoe-Missouria, Omaha, Dakota, Lakota, Kaw, Cheyenne, and Arapaho Peoples, as well as those of the relocated Ho-Chunk, Sac and Fox, and Iowa Peoples.

♾

Library of Congress Cataloging-in-Publication Data
Names: Towers, Paige, author.
Title: The sound of undoing: a memoir in essays / Paige Towers.
Description: Lincoln: University of Nebraska Press, [2023] | Series: American lives | Includes bibliographical references.
Identifiers: LCCN 2022042443
ISBN 9781496232878 (paperback)
ISBN 9781496235893 (epub)
ISBN 9781496235909 (pdf)
Subjects: LCSH: Towers, Paige. | Women authors, American—Biography. | Sound—Psychological aspects. | BISAC: BIOGRAPHY & AUTOBIOGRAPHY / Personal Memoirs
Classification: LCC CT275.T745 A3 2023 | DDC 612/.014453092—dc23/eng/20221129
LC record available at https://lccn.loc.gov/2022042443

Designed and set in Garamond Premier Pro by L. Auten.

For my sister, my parents, Kumar (my pockethand), and our dogs

We learn to live with [the noise] because we think that we must, but noise is and remains a disturbing element that reduces our quality of life. Not only for people, but for animals as well. I love waking up to birdsong, and there have been studies on how birds react to increasing noise levels in urban areas. The conclusion is that the songs of the birds have changed.

—Erling Kagge, *Silence: In the Age of Noise*

# Contents

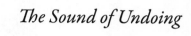

*The Sound of Undoing*

# Prologue
## *The Sound of Drawing* - - -

I remember her hands; they were tiny and pink. And her fingers, even at the age of eight or nine, still looked plump, like baby fingers, with sweet little shiny fingernails that her mother probably filed nightly. The way she moved her hands is what I can see most clearly though—so deliberate and graceful, as if she were a saleslady displaying an item of jewelry on the QVC channel. Like my older sister, my classmate (a now nameless girl who I can't pick out in a yearbook) had a way of making things beautiful.

In my few memories of her, she has a piece of paper placed on the table. First, she smooths the edges with her open palms, like she's prepping a canvas. Next comes the art tool selection process: she picks up a crayon, examines it, puts it back and chooses another. Every move she makes is serious and meticulous. By transient properties, everything she does becomes important.

And like an artist obsessed with a muse, my classmate also always draws the same thing: herself. Even the composition of her self-portraits remains unchanged.

After selecting a light brown crayon that best matches the color of her skin, she draws an oval—her head—that fills about three quarters of the page. The crayon doesn't lift off the paper, leaving an unbroken line. Next, she uses a black crayon to create the eyes (they look like loaves of bread—flat on the bottom, rounded on top) before drawing a large circle inside each loaf for the irises, two smaller circles for the pupils, and then coloring the pupils black, pressing down hard so that the wax becomes ink-like and glossy. Always, she leaves a dot of untouched white paper that looks like a reflection of light on the eye—an advanced drawing trick that all the other kids, including myself, now copy.

I

As much as I concentrate on watching her draw, I listen even closer. Unlike the squeaky *reet reet* of a marker or the fuzzy *iii-sss* of a pencil, a crayon has a softer, rounder sound, shifting with how much pressure one applies to the tool: a light shading or delineating produces the scratchy short vowel *a-aaa*. The destruction of more wax amplifies the *a-aaa* and then adds a low *eek eek* as the crayon is no longer pressed onto wood pulp, but instead onto another slippery layer of wax.

When the pupils are complete, my classmate uses the dark brown crayon to shade in the irises. I wish she'd also use a touch of olive green. Make them look like my sister's eyes. But she does color lightly here and the world becomes even quieter. Instead of that *eek eek*, this softened pressure emits a sound like the one made by running a fingernail across a piece of linen. Then comes my favorite part: she gently runs her palms over the crayons, searching for the hues that match her dress that day.

The crayons—most still cloaked in their wrappers—create a soft breathy sound when they're rolled, almost like water cresting and retreating, lulling me into a meditative state. Back and forth, back and forth, she's in no hurry. This isn't about the final product; it's about the experience. Thus, the second grade self-portrait becomes a performance art piece.

As strange as it may seem, these sounds—when combined with the visual triggers of careful hands and petroleum and pigment softening against paper—not only used to be a source of happiness for me as a child but also transported my mind and body into some sort of super relaxed high state. I didn't understand it then (and don't fully understand it now), but while watching her draw, it felt like dozens of downy feathers were tickling my face and the crown of my head. I slumped in my kid-size plastic chair, hands limp in my lap, head like a bobber on a fishing line, eyelids fluttering as sleepiness crept over me. My lips oozed into a smile.

This girl was not my sister, but in those moments, I loved her.

Now, I miss her. I wish to be soothed by the sound of her drawing. My sister no longer shares a table with me; I no longer hear that ridiculous high-pitched laugh that explodes from her mouth fast like a loon. Tell this girl to come to my house. I'll provide the art supplies. But tell her she still must be a girl so I can go back in time too. I understand that to draw is to sacrifice one thing for another. To use. To destroy. The sharp-tipped lead inside a pencil deteriorates, molecule by molecule, against paper. Chalk and charcoal crumble. Markers and pens bleed out until dry. Coloring, for the crayon, is a slow, tortuous process.

To create, we must break something else down.

Tell this girl I've been breaking down and I need her to take the place of the person I lost. No, who left me. I was just a child, *dammit*. Soothe me. Whisper in my ear. Tell her that all this destruction is audible, and it's so loud. Let's bring it back to crayons. Micro levels only. I am tired of the noise.

*Part*
*One*

# The Sound of Cutting

Cutting is both the action of something that cuts—like scissors—and someone who cuts something—like my older sister, who once cut her hair in front of the bathroom mirror at the house on Friendship Street while leaning over the sink, the dry severed hair crackling like fire. The nip of scissors is usually a clean, round, metallic sound—a light, snappy *ping*, or maybe a *tswchwing*—but my sister, inexperienced in all things fashion and beauty, closed the blades so slowly that you could hear every follicle being chopped, equaling one big *craaaww-swoosh*.

Trimming dry hair is a common practice now, but a professional will usually run the strands between two fingers and take short clips from the bottom up. Meaning, they don't just grab a section of hair near the forehead, hover the scissors parallel with the eyebrows, and say, "Here goes nothing."

Yet, at thirteen years old, my sister needed something new. She'd started by plucking her dark and prominent eyebrows into thin lines. Next there was a failed experiment with a box of blonde hair dye. (Afterward, she claimed that she'd wanted orange locks to begin with.) To me, the haircutting seemed like the most conspicuous act though. I waited in the hallway, listening through the door.

Upon reflection, I realize my actions were weird and intrusive. But this was my older sister, my best friend who sat next to me in a salon chair twice a year since I could remember. We were two girls draped in plastic capes making faces at each other in the mirror, maybe swinging our feet a little, while women wielding scissors chatted with our mother.

Now, this ritual had shifted. To cut your own hair meant that you had an opinion. It meant that you wanted to remake yourself and change the way you were perceived. This was intriguing but also, at the time, felt like a middle finger aimed at the natural way of things. For even when the bangs were *craaaww-swooshed* and the realization set in that they were short—very short—she sniffed and pulled her shoulders back, daring us to stare.

Over the following days though, I remember her tugging on the frayed ends in hopes that the hair would stretch and cover her eyebrows like she'd intended. On someone with glossy, straight hair, maybe you could conceal the mistake, but my sister was no slick-haired girl: her locks were dense, curly, and prone to expanding. But I never saw her cry about it; she has always been a master of self-preservation. She may have secretly laughed at herself, although she was probably aching over the thought of who she'd wanted to look like, who she'd wanted to be, *who*.

After a few months, the bangs reached past her sparse eyebrows and over her eyes and she hid behind this new fringe. Soon, there were also late nights and a diminished focus at school, but not in a way that seemed like a phase. Her behavior seemed riskier than that, as if in the process of enduring and then exiting childhood, she had been drained and now needed something to fill herself with.

She was searching and wasn't going to find what she needed at home, or even within her own self, meaning she certainly wasn't going to find it in me—the sister who loved her, who adored those moments when our relatives accidentally called me by her name, not my own.

We were a pair, I'd thought, a two-for-one deal.

I let this false perception linger all the way up until the day that she arrived home from that weekend-long Evangelical youth camp. Her bangs were grown out past her nose by then; her narrow face, I remember, reminded me so much of my own.

And she had her arms raised toward the sky, in praise of Jesus.

I'M SIX YEARS old. My sister is nine. We're in the back seat of the family car (it's a common scenario for us and will be for years to come) because we're driving home to Iowa after a trip out West. The winding highways of the Rocky Mountains have subsided and now the view from the rear window is middle-of-the-country monotonous. All I can see are flat fields and overgrown ditches.

Boredom overcame us hours ago.

We've already finished several run-throughs of a play between two stuffed animals. The plotlines and dialogue keep shifting: I thought there should be a murder, she thought someone should have a baby. The other games we play on road trips have lost their appeal too, like when we spot other cars with Iowa license plates.

We still have hours to go until we stop at a motel, but my sister has an idea: we should play hairdresser. She asks my mother for the foldable travel hairbrush that she keeps in her purse. It's shaped like an elongated seashell and when flipped open, one side contains a mirror and the other the soft, rubber teeth of the brush.

My sister is talented at making any game seem serious as she learned early how to mimic the behavior of adults. She puts her shoulders back, raises her eyebrows, and says things like "now look here" and "listen carefully" in this calm but assertive voice. Her lips are pursed in concentration; she takes pauses for dramatic effect. When she adopts this role of hairdresser, naming me her client, the result is more than entertainment—it makes me feel special, as if I'm somehow worthy of this expert attention.

The game lasts for at least an hour. She assesses my hair ("not bad but needs some work") while acting out a wash and cut. At some point, bobby pins and a rubber band are accrued, and she creates an "updo," and then pretends to spritz it with hair spray.

When it grows dark enough that we can only see the outlines of each other's faces, I adjust my seat belt, lie down, and put my head in her lap. She runs the brush through my hair until the tangles are gone and the rubber teeth comb through it like water. Listen: the shallow *swish* of waves. The brush grazes my scalp too and I grow sleepy. Still, she doesn't stop or push me away.

Sometime later, the glare of oncoming headlights scans my eyelids and I awaken in a motel parking lot. "We're here," she whispers, and her open hands are placed on my head, like a blessing.

THE RELIGIOUS CAMP my sister attended upon the invite of a school friend wasn't far from town. My parents, both lifelong liberal Methodists, figured that the weekend would consist of sing-alongs with guitars, games, prayer, platonic fun. But as soon as my sister walked through the front door, it was clear that something had changed: she hummed and sang her way around the house, acting like a person in love.

Serenading her movements with a half-hearted attempt at piano practice, I waited for my sister to notice me. Eventually, I lost patience and prompted her to tell me how lame church camp was, asking if she had to listen to some guy with a guitar lecturing about sin. Were the kids there weirdly enthusiastic? Did she have to participate in group activities?

Her gaze didn't meet mine and, even if it had, I wouldn't have been able to read her expression: Was she about to laugh or cry? Ignoring my questions, she said the weekend had been "amazing." She described scenes of praying, worshipping, and praise. She said she'd been "born again in Jesus's name."

At first, I listened. She had to be joking. But pressing both hands to her chest, she described the truths she'd heard, using phrases that weren't in her vocabulary two days prior—"the blood of Christ," for instance, and "our Lord and Savior." When she stretched her arms toward the popcorn-textured ceiling and declared her love for Jesus—as if I was no longer here, as if she'd entered a new plane of existence—my stomach sank.

Afterward, she didn't say, "I'm just kidding!" and wrap me up in a hug, and so I told her that she was acting strange, that she was scaring me, cut it out. I couldn't verbalize my dismay in any other way. My parents couldn't either and shrugged, thinking that this was just typical erratic teenage behavior. She'd mellow out.

Years later, I still wish that I'd told her that she didn't need saving—that she was enough on her own. Of course, it wouldn't have made a difference.

IN THE COMING weeks, I questioned how my sister absorbed the messages from this place, these people, without experiencing doubt. I challenged her, but it was like my voice—the one everyone mistook for hers on the phone—was inaudible. Instead, she left neon-colored booklets under my pillow. Among illustrations of the devil and stick figures with frowny faces enveloped in flames, the booklets warned readers of the dangers of hell in capital letters. I had to be saved by becoming BORN AGAIN in Jesus's name—it was the only way.

Other materials piled up around the house. One flyer expounded that the earth was only ten thousand years old, another discussed the myth of dinosaurs and evolution, and they all spoke of hell, sin, Satan, Jesus, and forgiveness.

My parents were upset, but she ran away each time they confronted her. At some point, I threw the booklets back at her, or took the scissors out of the drawer by the curly corded phone and cut them into dozens of pieces. The sound of the scissors slicing through thick paper was longer and deeper than the sound of cutting hair.

Soon, my anger became words. I explained things to her, condescended to her, wanted to shake her, called her "brainwashed" during at least one fight, probably more, and by the end of any confrontation, I found myself lacing up my shoes and leaving the house, swallowing my anger down until it was soothed by the quiet of the woods or the distraction of streets.

My coping mechanism was this: flee.

Still, the thing that haunts me most is that she thought she was doing right by me. She wanted to save her sister. And yet, I can't feel the love behind this act. I can only imagine a scene:

While I'm away, my sister opens my bedroom door and sneaks toward my small bed. Perhaps she notes the books on the floor, the felt-covered toy horses we played with as children, or my collection of journals, pressed leaves, and flowers displayed on my desk. Maybe the light is coming in through the window. Maybe she notices the photo of the two of us that I keep propped against my alarm clock. It was taken when we were maybe four and seven years old, and we're in a wooden fishing boat, ignoring the camera, caught in that moment right before laughter.

After entering this quiet space filled with the objects that represent me, or even smell or *feel* like me—her little sister—she still decides that I'm not enough. She still decides that the person who loves her most is destined for hell, for punishments more evil than imaginable due to what I'm lacking and what, within days, she believes she has found.

And, with a booklet in hand, she lifts my pillow.

I BEGAN CUTTING my own hair after college, bangs included. I like the ease of it and the ability to control the outcome, good or bad. The older I become, the harder it is for me to trust new people. Without receiving a professional haircut from time to time though, my hair— thick like my sister's—becomes unruly. Therefore, a few days before my thirty-first birthday, I made an appointment at a salon two blocks from my house in Milwaukee. I told the stylist that I wanted to take a few inches off and, also, could she make it lie flat?

As she trimmed, I closed my eyes for a moment and listened to the *ping* sounds. This relaxed me, and so we spoke a little about the heat and how we needed rain, and afterward she asked, "How long has it been since your last visit to a salon?"

It'd been over two years.

"At least six months," I said.

She laughed and told me that *it's fine*, but to try to come in every few months. I nodded: a lie.

As the stylist continued to cut—a playlist of eighties rock music playing on low volume in the background—she asked if I had family nearby. I told her that after years of living at least a thousand miles away, I now only lived four hours from my parents and two hours from my sister.

"Oh, you must see her all the time," she said.

"No," I replied, shrugging. "We don't talk."

Perhaps sensing intrigue, she asked why. I'd had this conversation several times before—with first dates, with friends, even on airplanes or trains while sitting next to talkative passengers. After years of silence, I allowed myself to admit to my non-relationship with the sibling people inquired about.

As she thinned the thickest sections of my hair with a razor, I told her about how my sister became a deeply conservative Evangelical Christian and how we fell out after that, sometimes going for years without speaking. My sister says that I was the one who left and that was true. I traveled, moved abroad, moved to the farthest reaches of the country, but she left first. Still, I always feel guilty when exposing her story. The facts are one-sided. It appears as if I'm the victim, as if she was the only one who did the cutting.

The stylist paused to examine her work and I blurted out, "I was really awful to her."

"Sounds like you had every right to be if she was as judgmental as that."

"Yeah, but I hurt her in return."

"Sorry, but she was the one who made the choice," she said and forced my chin higher with a firm hand. A moment later, possibly sensing my discomfort, she asked whether we'd ever reconcile. I told her about how we've tried on and off for years but that I was starting to wonder if it was impossible.

After picking the scissors back up, she frowned at me in the mirror, saying, "Well, sometimes you just have to cut toxic people out of your life."

I agreed with her but still wondered what had made me toxic.

BY THE TIME I was twenty-three, my sister had been married for a few years to a man she met through her church. He wanted to be a pastor; she wanted to be a pastor's wife. They eventually had four children. I didn't talk about her often, although I joked to friends while drunk or high that I was "lost" and she was "found." The contrast between our choices was jarring.

It did feel like I was going nowhere though: I'd spent most of college studying abroad and backpacking. I earned a bachelor's degree that I no longer wished to use, taught English in South Korea for a year as an excuse to wander rather than commit, returned to the U.S. and took up work as a temp office assistant in Denver, waiting tables on nights and weekends.

I wanted to be a writer, but I needed structure. Thus, I began a graduate writing program in Boston, thinking it would help me build a life filled with promise, not loss. Yet, during those two years of workshops in which I tried to write about anything else, I found myself turning in submissions about *her*.

This was deeply frustrating.

My essays would start with scenes in Vietnam or Peru or Spain, but then, without intent, there I was juxtaposing in memories of my sister's curly hair blowing in the wind on a lakeshore, or candlelight flickering across her face on the other side of the Ouija board, or the way she used to write the alphabet on my back with her fingertips. My sister would come to me like a phantom.

My parents, given no other option, accepted their changed daughter and even sat through services at her new church, but my sister and I didn't visit each other. We didn't call or write. Instead, our relationship came to a standstill that looked like this from both sides: I love you and thus I won't walk away, but I also won't make any move toward reconciliation because I won't risk being hurt any further.

The unknown makes everyone feel vulnerable.

For years, our mother told us that we needed to "move forward." She of course meant for us to be moving forward *together*, not just departing in disparate directions for good. She'd be devastated if one of her daughters interpreted her advice differently. Yet, my sister and I ended up fighting or crying every time we spoke.

When I browsed through photos of my sister's family online, all I could think was, in the future, these children might have the things I'd dreamed of over the years that have never come close to fruition for us, like: weekend visits where siblings stay up talking in hushed voices after everyone else has gone to sleep; phone conversations where she or

I only called to relay some funny thing that we witnessed on the subway, or in the park, or while out for a run—just any random story that serves as an excuse to hear each other's voice, to hear each other's laugh.

I missed her. But I also knew that I missed a defunct version of her—the person she was before being reborn.

SEVERAL YEARS AGO, while teaching a writing course, I read an essay draft from a student who visited an art museum with a friend. The piece appeared to have multiple themes; it was complicated, and she was figuring out what she wanted to express. But the part that intrigued me most in the piece was this strange, vague scene near the end that the writer couldn't seem to make meaning of.

It went like this:

The writer and her friend walked into a section of the museum that had antique furniture on display. Along the back wall of the exhibit, there was a wooden door that didn't have a sign of any kind on or near it. She noted that this seemed strange since museum doors are usually marked with instructions like Employees Only or Emergency Exit. But no, it was just a door leading to the unknown.

The two of them were so intrigued that they started to debate whether they should open it or not. (I like to imagine them conversing about it in nervous whispers.) They really wanted to—they couldn't walk away from it for some reason—but would they get in trouble with the security guard? Set off an alarm? Be kicked out? They paced the area for several minutes, unsure how to move forward.

Finally, the writer realized that it was possible to peer around the far corner of the exhibit's east wall. They'd be able to see what was on the other side without having to take the risk of opening the door.

What they witnessed on the other side of the wall was a massive, open atrium. Maybe sunlight filtered in through the cathedral-like windows and highlighted the sculptures on the white marble floor below. I don't know. But the discovery was jarring. If one were able to walk through this museum door, they'd just take a step out into the air, fall several floors down, and likely die.

With this insight, they hustled back toward the door and—hopefully now without hesitation—opened it. On the other side was just wall. The door was a piece of furniture displayed as part of the exhibit, like a memento of an entryway to a place that no longer existed. They felt foolish for having wavered for so long.

This brings me to another definition of cutting that has no physicality and thus no sound. After the cutting of ties has occurred, the world will be lonelier and quieter, exposing you to a louder *hum* of ambient noise (electric static, the distant barking of dogs, interstate traffic, a ticking clock) that only heightens with the realization that you'll forever be on the other side of that door. Whatever you two had has now ceased, has now stopped.

The only thing that can be done is to turn and walk away.

- - - - - - - - - - - - - - - - - - - - - - - - - - - - - - - - - - - - - - - -

### CAUSALITY

What does falling rain sound like before it hits the ground? Is the rain itself creating sound?

Water droplets collide, causing their molecules to combine in mid-air, yes, but this creates noise on such a minute level that humans are incapable of hearing it. What we hear instead is the sound of rain striking a surface: a single-paned window, a tin roof, the taut vinyl fabric of an umbrella, a car hood, a paved road.

Consider this well-known (perhaps excessively cited) poem from Bashō, the seventeenth-century Japanese haiku master:

The old pond
A frog dives
Sound of water

As noted in the book *Sound* by the French composer-filmmaker-critic, Michel Chion, the haiku challenges the idea of the mono-causality of sound. The frog is the action. The frog dove into the water. But neither the frog nor the water are the sole sources of the sound.

Humans are often quick to point a finger, to label, to find a single point. (This is bad. This is good. This is who's at fault. This was the cause.) In reality, of course, life is less sharply defined. A series of forces must combine—accidentally or not—to create an event. For instance, when we describe the sound of scissors, do we blame the blades or the strands of hair?

# The Sound of Control

In my elementary school friend's house, liter bottles of vodka were stored underneath the kitchen sink along with the sponges and dishwasher liquid. One afternoon, after spending the last hour in her above ground pool—a common activity that summer before sixth grade—I paused by the sliding door, wondering if it was safe to enter a place so loud. The TV was blasting commercials while my friend's mother sat on the couch, folding towels and stirring another Bloody Mary with a long spoon, oblivious to the noise. A moment later, her mother screamed at us to go throw our swimsuits in the dryer and so I took a deep breath and followed my friend inside to the laundry room, brainstorming excuses for why I had to leave.

Back upstairs, the commercials ended, and an episode of *Maury* came back on. My friend watched the TV upside down on the couch in a handstand, I sat tugging on my sleeves on a kitchen chair, and her mother sipped her drink, laughing—*no*, cackling—with the studio audience. I was waiting for someone to break and grab the remote. I was waiting for someone to take control of the clamor.

The television switched to commercials again and no one pushed the mute button. I felt sick to my stomach and stared at my knees. Folded towels were stacked on the carpet, one after the other, and my friend asked if I wanted to go to her room and I said *sure* but then changed my mind and said I should go home. I was tired. She tightened her lips and didn't respond. Tying my shoelaces in the front corridor, I felt her watching me from the stairs.

"We have ice cream," she said. A final plea.

"Thanks, but I'm not hungry," I lied. I knew she wouldn't speak to me for three days. I was leaving her alone with her drunken mother; I was leaving her alone. But outside on the peaceful street in the middle-class neighborhood of Iowa City, the relief I felt was as thick as chocolate syrup. I walked home smiling.

My friend's mother's alcoholism attached itself to this memory because the volume of the TV made no sense to me otherwise. To be loud, I thought, was to be unhinged. Loudness was a symptom of something bad. There needed to be a source for it—maybe vodka.

Now, I'm unsure whether the volume level of that TV was loud or just normal, given that I was unable to analyze decibel levels in the context of social norms until adulthood. In high school, for instance, I witnessed other friends' families enjoying (I wanted to write "allowing" here) sustained low or moderate noise in their homes. They turned on jazz or classical music or local radio and then just—
—*left it playing.*

To me, that was incredible. My family listened to music but it was monitored. No one let it play very loud for very long. Instead, we were a household of adjusters. Noise from the TV, radio, record or CD player was the occasional interrupter of the static goal of quiet. Virtuous, mindful, sensible quiet. Of course, the type of noise had to be tolerable as well. TV or radio commercials, for instance, were aural trash. So were mainstream talk radio, action movies, and music my father disliked, which was almost any album released after 1975.

From an early age, I also learned that to be quiet was to be wanted. This, of course, is an expectation placed upon most women, but in my home, the message was universal. To speak in a soft and calm tone, to take long pauses between talking—this garnered approval and access to my father, regardless of who you were. I needed to play it cool above all else.

My father's mood functioned like a volume dial. You play the wrong thing (or the right thing but too loudly) and you turned up his anxiety. During supper, my mother, sister, and I ate at the kitchen table, but my father sat in a recliner next to the table—a king upon his throne, plate in lap, facing the small television atop the counter that'd been manufactured before the invention of the remote. He chose what we watched—usually *The Andy Griffith Show* or *The Lawrence Welk Show*.

I liked these shows because he liked these shows. They were corny, quiet, and predictable, and he told stories about where he was when a particular episode premiered decades ago. Plus, the TV dictated our evening routine. In response to the occasional airheaded lines given to the actresses, my mother shook her head and said things like, "Oh my God, just shoot me now." We all laughed, but my father laughed the hardest, his face red and whole upper body shaking.

And yet, because my father is complicated, here is another memory: an episode of *Andy* cuts to commercials. TV stations play commercials louder in volume than the programs—this is a common complaint in my household. My father is at the stove grabbing second helpings of food and neither me nor my mother or sister get out of our chairs to hit the mute button in response to what we've been trained to recognize as undesirable noise. We're eating and talking and just don't react quick enough. Thus, my father sets down his plate, hustles to the TV, and slams the mute button with a stiff thumb, eyes glaring at my sister the whole time like, *Are you stupid? Are you that lazy?* His heated gaze shifts to the back of my mother's head, but she pretends not to notice. Somehow, maybe because I'm the youngest, I escape the blame.

Head down. Fork to mouth.

This scene is a composite scene because it happened so many times.

In the evenings, my father watched television in a recliner in the basement. Lights off or low. Beer or whiskey in a glass. I often joined him for a half hour or so to watch *The Joy of Painting with Bob Ross* or a clip of something new he'd recorded off the TV onto a VHS tape. Remote in hand, he monitored the natural rise and fall of noise with the volume button. Too loud dialogue: volume down. Too loud music: down.

Gunfire, hoof beats or a steamboat blowing its horn: down. If John Wayne's deep voice became too soft to decipher, he bumped up the volume, one push, two pushes, careful not to overdo it. *Oops* he over-did it: volume down. When the episode or clip finished, the TV was muted or lowered to whispers.

*Every* noise was assessed and controlled.

And this was my father in his most relaxed state.

In the modern world, chronic noise is, of course, universal. You can enter grocery stores, malls, airports, restaurants, bars, and elevators without experiencing a single downbeat of quiet, and my father was powerless when faced with this external soundscape, even in the polite state of Iowa. While he didn't mistreat those who were possibly responsible for the noise, like restaurant managers or party hosts, someone had to be an outlet for the bad feelings and your family is the easiest answer.

You can control a family because they love you. They need you. They adjust.

We chose restaurants based on their decibel levels, although going out to eat at all was a gamble. In places where conversation was lively and echoing, my father signaled that it was too loud by cupping his hands over both ears or pressing a fingertip against one ear like he was receiving a message. He frowned, avoided eye contact, and refused to join in the conversation. When my mother asked him if he was okay, he grimaced, as if her voice was grating his skin, and then mouthed the word, "What?"

He'd heard her. He didn't have any physical problem with his hearing. He faked deafness to emphasize the undesirable noise of this place we had brought him too. We could continue having a good time—thus becoming conspirators in his unhappiness—if we chose to.

Even if the restaurant was moderately quiet, he would bristle at, say, the brash voice or cackling laughs of a woman dining nearby. In those instances, I hated that woman too. *She* was the cause of my father's discontentment. *She* was why my father remained silent through this meal, simmered during the car ride home, jostled past us to get inside the house, and shut the basement door without saying "good night." I thought loud, talkative people were foolish and shameful. I felt embarrassment on their behalf.

My father's anxiety had weight and presence. It smothered. Even in a large public space, I could feel it like a heavy bass beating in your ribcage at a concert. It gave me headaches; it raised my heart rate. His anxiety was linked to the soundscape until it eventually became the soundscape, and the only way to break the bad feelings was to stop or lower the noise.

I thought this was my job—my impossible job. And so, by default, I also grew up believing his anxiety was my fault.

SO FAR, I have created a flat, sliver-size version of my father on the page. I wish to say: My father is magical. I've had dozens of people, young and old, mention how fortunate I am to have him in my life— this man who is so kind, unique, and funny. I've always thanked them and smiled in agreement because it's the truth. I am so fortunate. When my sister and I were young, he would adjust the record needle to the song "Part of the Plan" by Dan Fogelberg and turn the volume up. Heated up by the fast-paced melody, we sprinted across the carpet on the basement floor, back and forth, out of breath from joy.

I wish to say: My father took requests on nights he sang and played piano or guitar, and whenever he finished people begged for *another song, please*, because that is how beautiful his music is.

I wish to say: My father's quietness also taught me innumerable skills. He taught me how to fish. (Find a still, shady spot near the shore, don't make a sound, and wait.) How to tumble down deep into music instead of just treating it as auditory background. How to persevere. How to be still in nature. How to respect nature. How to feel the energy of trees through your palms. How to be reliable and self-reliant. How to listen to others. How to listen for birds, for deer, for car engine issues, for footsteps, for danger. How to listen.

But he also taught me that the world has a million audible triggers that altogether make up one massive minefield. After years of this, it becomes easier not to leave the comfort zone at all.

I first wrote this metaphor involving minefields as a trap instead. A cage. The feeling is the same. You're left with a man in his basement in Iowa monitoring volume levels on a television, controlled by his need to control.

AS AN ADULT, I'm trying not to smother others with my anxiety. That means I internalize. Thus, to protect myself as well, I'm working on an invisible sonar disc that deflects sound waves and acoustic-induced stress and shoots it all back into the universe. I call this shield, "It's Okay."

It has not always been okay.

In my late twenties, I moved from Boston to New York City with my husband, Kumar, who matched at a hospital on the Upper East Side for his medical residency. Manhattan is a strange choice of residence for a person who grew up swallowing noise like it was an enormous dry pill. I'd been training for this level of noise for the entirety of my young adult years though by traveling and living in major cities both abroad and in the U.S. I regarded these experiences as self-imposed exposure therapy—I didn't want to exist under the same limitations as my father. The modern world is loud, dangerously so. But without great social and political effort we cannot lessen it and, even so, at least noise is often accompanied by vibrancy and culture. There is new life, which breeds understanding. Thus, I learned. I grew.

And yet, in New York City—my biggest test—I failed.

Inundated with a chronic, inescapable, screaming cacophony of human-made sounds, noise pollution became the source of everything wrong. I lost control. My need for quiet became obsessive; I searched for it everywhere.

Even with its fenced-off fields, my first-choice destination, Central Park, was a haven but was also overrun by tourists. I'd find relief from the intense screech of air brakes on buses or rumbling garbage trucks but could still hear all that urban noise, even from inside the Ramble, which felt more like a tree museum than woods. The East River path did have a section that was peaceful at both dawn and dusk, but to reach it meant walking a mile along busy streets. Even Randall's Island wasn't free from the chronic *hum* of heavy traffic.

Soon, I could feel that *hum* in my bones. I could feel it in my blood and brain and soul.

I started mentally listing every unnatural noise and categorized each potential refuge by "how bad." My thoughts were obsessive:

If you stand among the boulders near the 102nd Street park entrance on a Sunday morning, it's quiet enough to hear the breeze rattling the leaves of the trees, but only until the city awakens at 6:30 a.m. ....

The Glen Span Arch near the Pool leads to a pathway that's less frequented and thus quieter, but on weekdays, you'll be bombed by construction noise . . .

In the evenings, the small stand of pines on the west side of Randall's Island dampens the distant sound of traffic on FDR Drive and the Robert F. Kennedy Bridge, but the patients pacing the fenced-in grounds of the Manhattan Psychiatric Center tend to stare . . .

Our own 450-square-foot apartment—our second rental in the city after I experienced a depressive episode in the first—had "giving spots" and "taking spots." One giving spot was the bedroom as its only window opened to the gap between our brick row house apartment building and the next. The outdoor deck—intended to be a small city sanctuary—was, surprisingly, a taking spot. Generators and window air-conditioning units droned so pervasively that the neighbors' trees were absent of birds. They couldn't hear each other's calls and I couldn't hear my own thoughts. A beer or three helped, as did popping a Xanax or chugging some Nyquil and passing out.

I was very tired. I aged a decade during those three years in that city.

There was a part of me that considered how it was unnatural to embrace the loudness. While people's sensitivities to noise vary greatly, it's clear that sustained exposure to high-decibel sound causes negative effects on a mass scale. I read books and articles about how noise pollution is responsible for hearing damage in millions of people around the world, not to mention elevated stress and blood pressure, disturbed sleep, lower birth rates, increased risk for heart attacks and massive negative implications on animals and the environment.

In other words, the ever-present undercurrent of my childhood was confirmed: chronic unnatural sound will hurt you.

But I recognized that my reactions to sound were spiraling out of control. Even low volumes of noise triggered my flight instinct. Thus, I developed tactics. I took deep breaths, centered my thoughts, shook out my arms like I was preparing for a run, and imagined myself like one of those inflatable tube men that I used to see twisting in the wind outside of car dealerships in Cedar Rapids.

"I'm easy-breezy," I told myself. "I will let this noise bounce right off of me."

But it didn't bounce off. Like my father, I'm imperfect. And thus, all that noise continued to trigger my anxiety, frustration, anger, and sadness, and I began to spew those bad feelings onto Kumar.

After a long day of being out in the city, I watched TV on low volume, beer in hand. If he pushed me to converse with him or asked me too many questions, I snapped and started arguments. I gave him looks like, *Are you stupid?* I was mean and controlled the environment of that tiny apartment with my instability. Here's the most shameful part: pulling him down to my level of stress-induced misery had similar effects to a shot of whiskey. It bought me a few minutes of relief to let off some of that pressure. It also left me deeply disgusted with myself. I was so sorry for how I'd treated my partner and best friend.

For the first time, I pondered what it took to release your noise-triggered anxiety on others. On your loved ones. It took a lot. Or was it that it took a little? Was it that it took almost nothing at all?

I vowed to stop and put myself in therapy.

I AM IN the car and the headlights from oncoming traffic highlight our faces, then our arms and torsos, then the tops of our thighs. It's summer and we're driving from Iowa to Florida for a week of vacation. I'm almost nine years old; my sister is eleven. My father is behind the wheel. The sun went down over an hour ago and we've arrived in our stopover city in Kentucky later than my parents had planned for.

Before the light dissipated, my sister and I had been calling out the states listed on license plates, searching for the most mysterious places, like Alaska and Maine. My father played his mixed cassette tapes because he controls the sound. A song came on that he liked, and he turned the volume up louder so he could sing along. His voice is soft and emotive. It is my favorite.

But now my parents are searching for a pre-booked motel and he's missed a turn and the car can't be escaped. We go silent. I lean over and whisper to my sister to ask her what happened, but she puts her hand on my knee and shakes her head *no.*

My mother is the navigator, so it is her fault. Not the missed turn— she'd told him at least three times that the left exit was coming up soon but he panicked trying to cross lanes and kept going straight. It's her fault because, earlier, after my father's tape ended, she'd turned on the a.m. radio to the classical music station. My father had clenched his jaw and squeezed the steering wheel as she fiddled with the dial. Afterward, he'd adjusted the volume down, then down again, looking over at her, his gaze hardened.

She'd ignored his hint to turn the music off though, instead tipping her head back against the passenger seat and humming along. Now, the tension in this tiny space is choking hot thick; now, we'll all be punished.

As soon as the car glides past the turn meant to be taken, he tightens every muscle in his body and punches the radio's power button with his thumb. His whole upper body lurches forward to kill my mother's music. The ensuing quiet pulses in my ears.

"*Goddamit,* I can't concentrate!" he yells.

My mother keeps her eyes forward, paper road map opened on her lap, pointing to the next exit sign on the right. She stays calm, even defiant, despite this massive mistake. Leaning forward, breathing heavily—panting, really—he takes the exit and follows it to a stop sign. At the stop sign, he curses and puts the car into park too fast and we all whip forward.

"Let me see this damn thing," he says and rips the map from her hands.

"Turn left," my mother says. Her voice is the first sound to break the quiet and it reminds me to breathe. He doesn't listen and instead slams on the overhead light, grunting, still cursing under his breath. The headlights of another car reflect in the rearview mirror and he panics again, punches the light off, throws the map aside, and puts the car in drive. He turns left, then left again—as my mother instructs him to do—then a right into the parking lot of the motel.

Once the car is parked, he taps his chest hard with outstretched fingers, spitting, "Never again! Never again!" His words are so booming that I clench my pelvic muscles in response to the sudden urge to pee. Then he laughs—not a genuine laugh, not the wheezing elated laugh that everyone else knows, but a loud fake mocking one. It's hilarious that we ever could have thought differently. *Hilarious!* His car. His rules. His music. How were we so stupid? *Never again.*

I struggle to undo my seat belt, my fingers fumbling with the button. The missed turn added maybe five minutes to the drive, but I'm both drained and beating with adrenaline.

Everything shifts at the sound of my sister.

"We're here!" she says in a gleeful voice.

"We're here," my mom repeats, her voice cracking with emotion but filled with gratitude for the angelic presence of her oldest daughter.

Sometimes I think my sister is invincible—I think she's immune to whatever it is I'm hearing. My sister is determined to look beyond the bad; she is always staring at the sky. Her energy changes mine, changes my mother's and mellows my heartbeat. Still, I can't shake it all away. At the *thwack* of my father slamming his car door, I flinch and then swallow, the sound of my own throat now magnified.

ONE EVENING LAST year, Kumar looked up from his plate and asked me what "too loud" is. We were sitting on the couch; I'd already finished supper and was scrolling through Yelp reviews of local restaurants on my phone. He'd watched me agonize for two weeks over where to take my parents to eat when they visited. We had relocated from New York City to Milwaukee for Kumar's gastroenterology fellowship earlier that year and I didn't know which places would be quiet enough. Now, he wanted an estimated volume level. He wanted to understand. This request surprised me because, no matter how many times I'm reminded, I still forget that we don't function under the same control panel.

"Too loud is too loud," I told him.

"Okay, I get that," he said. His patience with me is unbounded. "But do you see how that's subjective. Can you a give me some sort of idea?"

I paused, thinking the answer was when the volume of the noise triggers my father's anxiety—and it would be triggered immediately upon entering the space—thus subsequently triggering my anxiety. *That* was when it was too loud. I told Kumar some version of this and he nodded. But I realized later that night that this wasn't correct.

The right answer is the moment I hear the noise and feel afraid.

TO PLAY OR make sound in public is power. Consider nature's loudest noises: thunder, erupting volcanoes, and storms. Consider the Catholic Church's bells, pipe organ, and parades. Consider the drone and cacophony of capitalism's industrial machines, trains and factories and cars. Or men on motorcycles, men with chain saws, men with guns, men blasting music on the subway instead of using headphones. They subject us to noise without our asking. They steal our quiet. They feel ownership over public aural space.

Sometimes this takeover of public space is an act of rebellion and power after a lifetime of oppression, yes. Sometimes it's incredible.

But if noise is power, so is taking it away. Do it with anger and shame and it's a way of saying *shut up* without forming the words. It's a hit, not to the face, but in some ways the violence feels the same. To hit is to transfer weak, unstable energy—not just cause stinging pain. You didn't ask for this energy, you didn't deserve it, but now it's here, pulsing in your body. You're at the mercy of someone else.

My father controlled the spaces we shared with him through his reactions to and requirements for sound. The empathetic view of this reality is that my father had terrible, undiagnosed, and untreated anxiety—untreated mental illness—that was sparked by noise, among many other lesser factors. The empathetic view is that he experienced this control at the hands of his own father, except on a far worse scale. Another view of this is that he made a choice. He made choices. We couldn't control the sound of the outside world. We couldn't control. But noise became tangible—so swift was its conversion from invisible vibrations and waves to anxiety to a knot in my throat so tight that I was forced into silence for years.

Still, I wish to say: when his anxiety isn't at the wheel, my father is one of the most wonderful people you'll ever be fortunate enough to know.

*Dad, if you're reading this, I am so sorry.*

THE FIRST TIME I got into a car with Kumar, he drove. We were headed to the convenience store to pick up energy drinks to ease our hangovers and then going out for lunch. Kumar was just my roommate then—he'd moved into my apartment in Boston a week before as a subletter. I was finishing my MFA, he was nearing his final semester of medical school, and we'd become instant friends. In the car, he told me to play whatever music I wanted to. I froze. Few people had granted me that gift before. Only, I didn't see it as a gift: I saw it as a setup. I selected a song from one of the playlists on his phone and lowered the volume just as it was starting. He reached out his right hand and turned the dial up.

*His decision—not my fault*, I told myself.

But I grew quiet anyway.

Driving north along Centre Street in Jamaica Plain, he couldn't find a place to park. He slowed in front of an opening that turned out to be a "loading only" zone and I gripped the door handle. The music was overwhelming. My throat tightened. He touched my knee and told me to relax.

A block down, I spotted another open space and yelled out, but it was too late to back into it—there was a line of cars behind him. He shrugged and turned right onto a side street so he could circle around. The music played through all of this stress at the same volume. Strangely, I could feel my muscles unclenching. The sound swept me up, made me feel both energetic and relaxed.

"See? It's okay," he said after parking.

"It's okay," I repeated, as if testing out the words, feeling them shape and form power in my mouth. The words were sounds that I hoped to eventually speak without hesitation. *It's okay, it's okay, it's okay.*

- - - - - - - - - - - - - - - - - - - - - - - - - - - - - - - - - - - - - - - - - - -

### SICK

Centuries-old books, letters, journals, and other texts prove that, even well before the raucous rise of the industrial era, there was a clear correlation between noise and irritation. In fact, it's so clear that irritation is sometimes established as "a given" in scientific studies on the relationship between noise pollution and mental illness. Over time, an irritating acoustic backdrop cannot only cause stress, anger, frustration, and increased blood pressure; numerous studies have also linked noise pollution to increased anxiety and depression, as well as heart disease and stroke.

Meaning, noise pollution—which is now prevalent in cities, towns, and rural areas around the world—is so pervasive and unnatural as to harm humans, even when they're sleeping.

In 2016 a study from the University Medical Center of the Johannes Gutenberg University Mainz in Germany found that people who expressed a strong annoyance with the noise pollution in their area experienced a twofold higher prevalence of depression and anxiety than the general population. People who lived in neighborhoods with significant aircraft noise were particularly susceptible to mental illness.

Unfortunately, children also are vulnerable to the consequences of the chronic thunderous hum of modern societies. In 2018 researchers from Ulsan College of Medicine in South Korea published a study on how noise pollution affects elementary and middle school students. Both chronic noise pollution exposure and noise sensitivity were found to be significantly associated with "internalizing and externalizing" problems. These problems included anxiety, depression, a diminished level of self-control, and shorter attention spans.

Why is noise making people so sick? This link between noise pollution and mental illness is likely due to our ingrained "fight or flight" response. A chain saw rumbles and the amygdala—an area of the brain responsible for emotions and survival instincts—sends an SOS to the hypothalamus. This hormone-releasing region of the brain then signals the adrenal glands, which release the body's stress hormones, adrenaline and cortisol, thus spiking the heart rate and blood pressure.

Stress hormones, of course, are meant to be deployed in life-threatening situations. So, when one's body senses noise pollution as a threat, over and over again, it can lead to burnout. This burnout can then lead to breakdown. It's no wonder that some acoustic researchers refer to this cycle as "decibel hell."

In the conclusion of the South Korean study about how noise is harming children, the researchers wrote that, "Noise is an inevitable problem in modern societies" and urged that the focus needs to be on strategies for treating children affected by their polluted environment—not on the noise itself. This is sad but not shocking. Many people, including physicians, scientists, and public health officials, view noise pollution as a chronic, unsolvable problem that we can only react to, instead of mitigate or fix.

# The Sound of Awakening

"Waking up doesn't sound like anything," an imagined voice tells me.

This voice belongs to a man, the type of man who only shakes other men's hands at parties, and I don't like authoritative statements. Or sexism. Meaning this invisible contrarian has served his purpose; I want to prove him wrong.

Some people might assume that awakening doesn't have a sound, given that it's an internal act, a brain act, and the micro noises of the fluttering of eyelids or the *click* of a shifting sleep-stiff neck are just the consequences of one silent switch being turned ON. But I argue that there's a unique vibration between *asleep* and *awake*, because these states of consciousness do not exist like distinct realms where, from your bed or couch or mat, you silently → into the other realm in nanoseconds with no lingering—no whisper—of the one left behind.

The transition is more fluid than that.

An obvious metaphor to demonstrate the sound of awakening would be to submerge you underwater and then have you rise to the surface, zeroing in on that moment when you break through the water's skin, that moment before your ears have popped, and the voice of your sister calling your name is dampened and distant even though there she is: right at the edge of the lake.

But this isn't exactly how I perceive it—some internal rhythm is missing, some deeper level of complexity. Instead, you must be taken to the inner horizontal layer of a forest, past the sparse, skinny trees that grow along the perimeter; past the grasses and bushes and thorns bathing in sunlight; past the raucous birdsong and the screech of cicadas; and toward the timeworn, massive hardwood trees, or the haunted softwood pines—so sprawling and dense that they hinder the light from reaching the ground, and thus underfoot there is just cool, hard-pressed dirt, moss, ferns, dead leaves, pine needles, and quiet. Lie down there and press your ear to the earth.

IT WAS A late spring evening in Iowa when I walked out the back door of my parents' house and descended into the woods. No one questioned where I was headed. I was seventeen years old; the answer was always "out." I crossed the creek at the bottom of the ravine by sidestepping across a fallen log and then followed a deer trail that cut through the brush up and over several hills. The family cat, a gray tabby, shadowed me from a distance, his paws picking through the undergrowth as if one wrong step equaled death.

After a half mile, the thorns and thickets fell away and opened into a flat area of much taller, older trees, the smallest of which was in bloom with velvety white flowers. The light, still hovering above the canopy line, appeared to be filtered through honey-yellow stained glass—causing even the weeds to seem charmed—and I stood there waiting for the cat's arrival, thinking of my sister.

For most of my childhood, my sister walked with me to and from school. She accompanied me to the park, to the creek and the cement tunnels under the bridge, to the vacant fields east of our neighborhood. She even accompanied me to the bathroom: we liked making a game of who could pee for the longest continuous amount of time.

I'd forgotten this and stood there in the cool stillness, smiling at a memory of her standing by the bathtub with my mother's kitchen timer, yelling for me to start. We'd both already chugged two large glasses of water in preparation.

Now I was alone in the woods and nearly finished with high school and she was three years moved out of the house, although one could say she was gone before she packed her belongings into boxes and suitcases. The endless hours we spent together had shifted into months apart, as they often do between siblings. The elder reaches the age of self-assertion and independence; the younger sits outside the elder's closed bedroom door, trying to catch snippets of a gossip-filled phone conversation.

*What has changed?*

It's a common inquiry from the younger siblings of the world. Yet, as I stood there among the trees, it became clear that I'd lost more than my relationship with my sister. I'd also lost my sense of security in the outside world. My sister took a right turn without even a *good-bye*, leaving me facing an onslaught without my shield. In my new teenage body, men stared at me as I passed by. It's as if they weren't seeing my humanness. I could no longer move through the world as if it was also still mine.

A slight wind jostled the highest branches of the trees as the cat and I reached the clearing. Rubbing his face against my shins, he vibrated with purrs before freezing at the overhead cry of a bird—his pupils blackening as if foreseeing possible violence. And I remembered how my sister had started to cut her own hair, how she was taking control of her body, maybe in response to something being taken from her.

She chopped a thick fringe of bangs right there in the bathroom mirror late one night while I spied on her from the hallway, thinking, *Since when do we cut our own hair?* I hadn't yet realized that there was no longer a "we."

The next day, I picked up the scissors she left on the bathroom counter and contemplated the way my hair looked like a child's—wild, tangled, three days unwashed. Perhaps that is when girls stop being girls: when they don't just see but also see themselves as they are seen.

I cut off three inches.

Soon, feelings of isolation settled in. I missed my sibling. I missed my old self, the child I was when I was with her. Because when you see yourself from an outsider's perspective, it chips away at your freedom. First, this altered view hovers around the fringes, but then it spreads toward the core.

You lower your gaze to the ground when passing watchful eyes——or freeze in reaction to a twig breaking.

You think about how someone might interpret your body, or what they might want or try to do to your body.

Meaning, even when you are alone in the woods, reaching out to touch the tips of the verdant ferns as you pass by, you remain restricted.

MY DREAMS HAVE always been vivid, but one year in high school, a friend gifted me a dream diary. I can better recall those dreams that I fleshed out with words. That, and when scanning over the entries from that period, a pattern emerges. Most of my dreams contained two themes: 1) loneliness and 2) exposure.

Around the time that my sister stopped acting like my sister, I dreamed about walking along a dirt trail that cut through a forest where the trees grew just a few inches apart. It was very quiet outside. Maybe it was even silent, and silence—universally lauded for its peacefulness—is simultaneously oppressive *and* capable of stripping you of any feeling of protection. Without the cover of sound, even as gentle as the chiming of water, it's as if there's no place to hide.

The light was dim. I told myself not to panic, but I was desperate to find open land. Finally, the small gaps between the trunks widened, but once I followed the trail around a bend, I saw a man standing in the trail maybe forty or fifty feet ahead. He was motionless. Staring. I kept walking toward him, instead of doing what my body ached to do: run. I remember thinking, *I don't want to be rude.* Yet, when I came closer, I noticed how his eyes were narrowed.

According to my diary entry, I said something like, "I need to go find my sister," as if this stranger deserved an explanation for my behavior. But when I spun around, intending to take off in the direction I'd just come from, I found that the trees had rearranged themselves even tighter together, creating an impenetrable wall. I had no choice but to turn and face this man on my own.

Even though I woke up before any violence occurred, the whole scene stuck with me for days. Although I couldn't describe exactly what was going to transpire, I instinctually knew that I would give and he would take, no matter how much I fought against it, and I would leak or maybe eventually hemorrhage from all that giving and taking, thus devolving into some emptied-out shell of my former self.

My sense of vulnerability spiked afterward. I couldn't even muster the courage to shuffle down the hallway to the bathroom at night. I lied awake in bed, my bladder aching. Only the soft nudges from the cat felt safe.

I don't have any memory of hearing the sound between asleep and awake during this period of my life. I snapped in between those two states rapidly, as if my survival depended on it.

IN THE WOODS behind my parents' house with the cat and the trees and the warm touch of sunlight, a thought occurred to me: *I could just stop here and nestle myself into the dirt.* The cat sprawled across my feet, exposing his belly. I decided I'd go with the feeling but realized, as well, that I needed to be naked.

At the age of seventeen, just the lying down felt like an act of rebellion. How often do girls, much less women with grown bodies, just stop and go facedown on the ground? And to deepen the rebellion further by getting undressed outside, among the trees, felt provocative, strange, perhaps even dangerous—so much as to be intoxicating, as if I had just discovered that I could float away from this post-adolescent life and enter a new realm where my body was just a body, not to be touched or leered at or obsessively examined but just to be.

I untwisted the rubber band holding my hair back in a ponytail first.

After that initial letting down, I tore off anything that wasn't a part of me. I tugged my hiking boots off and set them aside, not bothering to tuck in the laces or stuff my socks in the holes. While undoing my stopwatch and silver locket necklace, I noticed the piece of worn, yellow ribbon that I'd tied around my wrist—my sister used to wear it in her hair as a child—and undid that too. Then I lowered myself to the ground and took a shaky breath before pulling off my T-shirt and sports bra.

Finally, after shifting my weight onto one hip, I pulled off my jeans and underwear.

Once I was naked, I stood up to prove to myself that I could be this unabashed, that I could be as free as an animal, before lowering back onto my knees. The cat sat a few feet away atop a protruding tree root and groomed his front paws, averting his dark green eyes, as if out of respect. I brushed away the broken acorns and dead leaves in front of me, then brought my body down onto the cool, damp ground. My arms braced the earth like a "t," my neck was twisted at an uncomfortable angle and, from this low, all I could see was the base of the nearest tree, stray strands of grass, and my outstretched fingers.

I'd never witnessed another person in these woods and, either way, the undergrowth was so dense that the cat and I would hear someone coming. Yet, I fought a constant, boiling urge to sit up and scan the trees for a potential predator, like that man who'd followed alongside me in his car while I was on a run one Sunday morning. (He had leaned out the window and licked his lips as if I was only alive in *his* world and thus something to be caught.)

I also worried that another person picking their way through this cut of land would spot my supine figure in the trees and mistake me for dead. Or crazy. Still, I didn't rise. I remembered another game I used to play with my sister: first one to twitch loses. It was difficult to win in the summers when the black flies and mosquitoes swarmed.

The longer I lied there in the quiet, the less I seemed to exist, which was what I needed, because at that time I was just a girl transitioning out of one stage of life and into the next. Like most, I feared this involuntary transformation. I was struggling (flailing) with the in-between. As I'd aged, my world had narrowed and darkened until I felt as if I'd been cut loose from the earth. It'd never occurred to me that along with the sudden importance of what I wore and how I looked and the embarrassments and fears and bad dreams that there'd also be a loss of the most basic connections: Like, me and my sister, me and nature, miniscule (me) and immense (whatever life is).

I was taking back whatever connections I could.

I didn't understand why my new body seemed to innately attract danger and shame, but here, unwatched in the woods, I freed myself from those dreadful hooks attached to what was just flesh, blood, bone, skin, and hair. After a few minutes, I stopped reacting to every micro noise. My instincts took over and neutralized my fear. With one long inhale, I turned my head further to the side and put my ear to the ground. My heartbeat slowed. I quit thinking, quit obsessing, and sunk into how I really felt: both empty and full.

Then the sound came.

The sound is the sound of the in-between, an elusive state I've only experienced this one time by my own will. It's also an internal sound, only able to be heard within the body, and thus not cognized as "sound" by another listening ear. Still, I've heard it.

It lies in the vast state between abstract and quantifiable. But it also increasingly beats with blood and force as you get closer to consciousness, as if it's willing you to push off and embrace the noise of life. Anything and nothing can exist there if you just figure out how to stay floating in the rift.

There's no pulse in the forest, no thump or rumbling. But what I did hear was a constant *o-oooohhhh* or *m-mmmmm* that was so rounded, so ancient, that it penetrated my senses, like one of those full body massage chairs rich people always seem to have in their homes—have you tried those?—they shake everything loose until you can't even close your own gaping mouth.

The feelings of loss loosened too and now I could sense how the *o-oooohhhh* was simultaneously a deep groan *and* the whistle of air blown over an open bottle, meaning I was upheld by something big and warm and solid, while also floating past high schools and locker rooms and hospitals and churches and men in cars in the cold, crisp air. I could live forever in that lulling sweetness if only I could let go a little more, if I could let that *m-mmmmm* just take me in . . .

AND NOW:

Take the hum of a forest floor and mix in a few unidentifiable voices leftover from a dream, the sound of wind rattling dry leaves that have fallen in one world and not the other, your mother sliding open the screen door to let the cat out, your sister passing your bedroom door on the way to the bathroom (she's trailing a finger along the wall), and bring it all up slow, like a conductor raising her arms for a crescendo, those last *ooooohhhhmmmmmm* moments between the sound of sleep and the sound of consciousness, and with it bringing your own internal voice saying, *oh fuck, it's morning*, and then snap your fingers.

You have now awakened.

- - - - - - - - - - - - - - - - - - - - - - - - - - - - - - - - - - - - - - -

### THERAPY

Sound can heal.

Sound is touch.

Sound has tones and melodies that open a pathway to the divine.

These are all claims from sound healers and therapists.

Music therapy, long praised by both medical and holistic communities, has been shown to lower heart rates in patients, including infants. Hospitals even employ certified music therapists (who use instruments such as reverie harps, guitars, drums, and their singing voices) to reduce the stress and pain of cancer and surgical patients.

As documented by the late author and neurologist Oliver Sacks in his book *Musicophilia*, music is also able to penetrate the part of the brain that controls memory and emotion. Patients with dementia, Dr. Sacks writes, can experience improved moods, cognitive function, and motor movements from listening to old-timey songs.

There's more evidence on the therapeutic qualities of sound: A 2016 observational study done by researchers from the University of California in San Diego showed significant reductions of tension, anxiety, depressed moods, and pain after undergoing a sound mediation session using singing bowls. Forged from copper, brass, or other metals, these bowls produce a deep, penetrating "ring" after being struck or scraped with a mallet. They were used for therapy as early as the twelfth century and are still used for Buddhist rituals and meditation in Tibet.

Additionally, research has shown that chanting, in combination with meditation, reduces stress and pain, decreases anxiety and depression, improves sleep, and lowers blood pressure. Sound healers now even use tuning forks to create vibrations that "touch" certain areas of the body, like acupuncture, or offer immersive "sound baths" using crystal bowls or didgeridoos.

Still, while research, methods, schools, and recognition from the medical community have legitimized the healing power of music, research on sound's connection to the physiological is limited in other areas. Therapies and healing methods trend in popular holistic culture and the benefits are often based on testimony or shared beliefs. But it's clear that transporting people back to their basic senses using sound may allow them to hit an invisible "reset button," or at least help them to transcend some of the pain of being alive—if only until the music stops.

# The Sound of a Loon Call

Imagine a step stool: small, basic, plastic, or wood. Unfold it and set it on the floor. Now jump onto it if you're able—both feet at once—and hop up and down three times in quick succession. Jump back down to the floor and then up onto the stool again for three more hops. Repeat. Repeat. Listen to how the tone of the three hops on the stool is higher than the heavy thump against the floor that bookends them.

Now, take that rhythm—*boom, bum-bum-bum, boom*—and triple, maybe even quadruple the speed of it. Add musicality, like the blow of a two-toned, high-pitched whistle, and magnify those rapid five bursts of sound over an expansive clear lake in northern Minnesota, listening to it bounce off the water and echo against the dense borders of pine trees. Let there be a darkening sky flushed at its edges with the remnants of sun. Let there be a cool fog rising.

This is the tremolo call of a Common Loon.

Those who live in northern areas inhabited by these black-and-white spotted and striped water birds often describe this pattern as "laughing." If you really listen, though, you'll hear the stress and urgency behind those fast expulsions of air. A tremolo call is used to warn and communicate distress, like when a nest of chicks is threatened, or territory is encroached upon, or when a loon is startled by a child in an orange life jacket perched on the bow bench of a fishing boat, pointing and whispering, "Look, look, look!" to her older sister.

When my father took us out on the water in Minnesota, this was the usual noise the loons made in our vicinity, or just a hoot or yodel. Sitting sideways in the back of the boat, he steered with the lever attached to the gas motor and killed the engine once we were out of ear's reach of the shore.

My sister and I grew lethargic from the sound of the loons and breeze-blown waves lapping against the sides. Still, we were trespassers—quiet and contemplative ones for the most part, but aliens eliciting tremolo calls, nonetheless.

It wasn't until nighttime, back on land, when we heard them wailing.

The wail of a loon is reminiscent to a wolf howl or owl hoot. These sounds are haunting and melodic. Mournful. They empty an animal of air. Like music, the continuous rising and falling note, purer and fuller than any flute, also triggers tingly skin and rising arm hair. You may sink on land from all that serotonin dripping down your spine. The world feels wider; the world feels not the world but instead one ripple in an infinite universe and, yes—*ha!*—of course your soul will continue to be after this body is gone. You know it now.

But who is to say whether loons feel emotionally or spiritually moved by their own wailing? Is unworldly beauty the intention? Meaning, one set of ears may hear, *hey I'm over here where are you,* while another set of ears hears God.

MY SISTER WAS born in Iowa. I was born in Minnesota. We lived near a lake (most Minnesotans do, as the state holds twelve thousand lakes) for the first six years of my life until my parents moved us south to the cornfields of my sister's birthplace. We were raised to like water; we grew up on the sound of loons.

We were also raised to be religious. My parents are both from Methodist families in rural and small-town eastern Iowa. This match wasn't uncommon—Methodism is the largest Christian denomination within the heavily white Protestant state. We went to church every week because that's what people did.

Inside, ushers manned the opened doors, reciting the word "welcome" as they handed out that day's pastel-colored pamphlet. People greeted each other in hushed voices drowned out by the organ playing funeral music.

"Peace be with you," they said.

We responded, "And also with you."

Halfway through the service, the pastor called on the children to leave for Sunday school. We rose from the wooden pews and followed women who were not our mothers outside the sanctuary, across the corridor, and down a hallway. My sister and I often made a game out of coordinating our footfalls; I remember the synchronous *tap tap tap* of our Mary Janes.

Wooden-framed portraits of a doe-eyed white Jesus and laminated posters that stated, "Praise the Lord!" in bubble letters hung in the classroom. The teachers distributed illustrated story packets printed on flimsy recycled paper. Each Sunday was a new packet: Noah leading animal couplets up a wooden ramp and onto the ark. Jesus washing a woman's dirty feet. The three wise men gazing across perfect hills of sugar sand. In the center of the table sat Tupperware containers of used crayons and pencils, and we colored in pictures of Joseph standing over his virgin wife while she cradled another man's son or wrote answers to basic comprehension questions printed on the last two pages.

"What sacrifices did Cain and Abel make to God?"

"While inside the belly of the whale, what did Jonah pray about?"

Down the hall, across the corridor, and through the closed doors of the sanctuary, we could hear the adults singing, or the garbled words of the pastor, punctuated by a microphone. I disliked coloring in those packets with the dull wrapperless crayons; the soft paper tore and the usual crisp sound of writing with a pencil was dampened. My sister didn't seem to care. Smiling, she listened to the women in earnest.

But after twenty minutes of biblical story time, several children would start shifting in their seats and the teachers spoke louder in response to the loss of attention. A sense of anarchy licked the air and just before all focus was lost, it was time to line up at the door and walk nicely back to our parents.

After the service ended, the adults erupted into conversation. Women laughed and worked the room; men slapped each other on the back. Next to the main gathering area was a large kitchen staffed by women-only volunteers. Stainless steel vats of coffee appeared, as did Styrofoam cups, packets of sweetener, tiny containers of cream, and boxes of powdered sugar doughnut holes. All the kids darted around the adults' legs to grab doughnuts; my sister could fit three in one hand—one for me, one for her, split the third.

The sugar and post-service freedom flowed, and my sister and I spun in circles on the sidewalk during the walk to the car. At home, we stripped off our dresses and danced in our tights. Even though the constricting legwear left indentations on our skin for hours afterward, we didn't shed it: while sliding across the linoleum floor in the kitchen, I could almost hear the rumble of rebellion.

We'd sat still and listened all morning like good girls. A man in robes lectured and told stories that had to be bent, repackaged, and sucked dry for meaning due to the imperfect mortal text they came from. Now we were naked from the waist up, flaunting our imposed undergarments, our encased legs no longer pretty but instead funny, like little sausages.

Here is my understanding of those Sundays: religion was community was the morally right thing to do was the expected thing to do. It was the healing balm and deeper meaning to a white suburban or small-town way of life. This was also the Methodist church: No one was a zealot or a pusher. No one worshipped God or Jesus with an external display of emotion. Intolerance was also more carefully disguised than other denominations. And after we changed into street clothes, ate lunch, and washed dishes, my sister and I ventured outside, back into nature, back to the water, to birdsong, back to what made sense. At least for me.

THE SUMMER THAT we moved out of Minnesota, I wandered our new backyard in Iowa like Moses in the desert, searching for water and the signs of life that relied on it: the blistered toads, the croak of bullfrogs, the damp soil smell of earthworms, rainbow-scaled carp, the nighttime wail of the bird that made me believe in God.

Loons do not live in Iowa.

It was during this period of adjustment that I experimented more with sound. I see now that this was a self-soothing technique. I could mimic a loon's tremolo call on my mother's kitchen stepstool. *Boom, bum-bum-bum, boom.* My sister worked with me for years on the art of whistling, but I couldn't mimic more than a screaming teakettle. Thus, like a pianist breaking down each note in a chord, I matched and sang the notes of a songbird's multitoned vocalization one at a time instead. Quiet noises produced by mundane actions, like the brushing of hair (running water) or the crackling of a plastic grocery bag (campfire), relaxed me if I could slow my mind enough to listen to them.

It was difficult to slow my mind.

But my sister helped. She was forever tolerant of the anxiety that overtook me around other people, as well as a growing sensitivity to noise that stressed me to the point of shutdown. One morning in church, I couldn't calm my agitation from the sound of an elderly man behind us clearing his mucous-clogged throat every ten seconds. She took me by the arm out of the sanctuary and into the bathroom. Behind the safety of a closed door, she demonstrated how to fold a paper towel into a tiny pocket triangle. I remember the quiet breathy sound of her fingers against the paper. I remember my deep relief and gratitude. My sister: the savior.

I relied far too much on one person, one child, for my happiness and security. I see that now.

By the age of twelve, I refused to attend church most weeks. My father stopped going as well. We had all played our roles. Now only my mother and sister pulled on tights or pleated pants on Sunday mornings.

I had analyzed the stories, the actions and messages, and then— *poof*—the magic was gone. I felt I'd been hoodwinked by the Bible's Old English words—the thous, thys, haths and hath nots—and the almost indecipherable footnoted text on diaphanous sheets bounded by leather. Its ancient status alone inspired awe. That, and the customs, the clothes, the standing up and sitting down, the altar and cross, the conditioned respect, the pipe organ, the repeated words of prayer, the mystery. I loved the peacefulness of prayer, but I could clear my mind in other ways and places. Specifically, being outside.

Every pastor I'd encountered spoke with the same cadence, with rises, falls, and rhetorical questions, with pauses broken by his own voice and well-placed jokes. A talent honed with observation and practice. If he could get his congregation to laugh and expel their discomfort and apathy, then he earned their vulnerability and could stick them with meaning, shame, guilt, and fear. This sounds malicious and it can be. But I sensed it was often done with good intent.

Of course, writers and storytellers do the same thing: they earn your trust and then swoop in with a knife.

But here is the other possibility: I am wrong. I didn't realize it until I was an adult, but even as a young child, my sister was devout. She listened to the whispers of *amen* and heard something beautiful and limitless. I witnessed the way she clasped her hands in prayer; it was so natural as to appear to be guided by the divine—not automatic trained behavior. She was skin tingling and arm hair rising; she was all in.

And while dancing in tights was a *get a load of this shit!* act for me, upon reflection, I think it was another genuine celebration of Sunday for her.

My sister eventually questioned religion too, just not the source of our gathering. Rather, she doubted the interpretation and delivery. By her early teenage years, she was increasingly private, morose, and always mimicking the behavior and appearance of whoever was in closest proximity. She was strong but swayed. She also had a respectful yet apathetic attitude toward school that's hard to specify. Her report card listed decent grades but she ghost-walked through each class or activity, *trying* to feel ignited—my God, she was trying—but she mostly just survived. Existed. Unlit.

At the age of fourteen, another church provided a new under-standing for her. Evangelicalism is intense, intoxicating, persuasive, and poured over you instead of administered like a warm drink. It's self-driven—a one-to-one relationship with Jesus. Instead of a community striving toward what they gauge to be a better and more stable way of life, congregants become Christian soldiers. Fear pulses and is soothed with the one and only answer for how to get to heaven. For how to live a life. Severe and less carefully hidden intolerance is justified as truth. *So says the book.*

When she went away for a weekend Evangelical church camp with a friend, my parents knew only of Methodist and Lutheran youth groups. They never imagined it could be much different. But she came back carrying pamphlets damning her family to hell if they didn't accept Jesus as their savior. She came back fully submerged.

Considering the encompassing power and love of born-again Christianity, perhaps that is the largest flaw of milder denominations: they are easy to leave. And yet. I refuse to believe that it was easy for my sister to leave me. It's just that past ties that hinder a baptism in deep water must be severed.

The part of me that pushes too hard wants to include a memory here of her fastening me into my life jacket before climbing into a boat roped to a dock in Minnesota. I know it's excessive. But I still wish to say that she always put mine on first. I have no memory of tightening her straps with my smaller hands and I regret that.

IN MY SENIOR year of high school, my parents and I went to a service at my sister's adopted church in Iowa City, where she attended college. I sat in the back seat of the car, arms crossed over my chest. I'd avoided this day until the need to witness overcame me. On a Sunday several months before, my parents had walked through the garage door with sullen faces—my father in a suit coat, my mother in a blouse and skirt.

"How was it?" I asked.

"It's a little different than what we're used to," my mother said.

Her words were chosen carefully, as if slowed by shock. My father pursed his lips and escaped to the basement for the rest of the day. I was curious but scared. I didn't push her for more answers.

On the morning I decided to go with them, my father followed a line of cars turning into the church's parking lot, which could have accommodated a mass procession of pilgrims. The Methodist church that only my mother now attended had a congregation dominated by elderly people. But here, families and young people crossed the expanse of pavement as if pulled toward the open front doors. We followed them.

This memory still feels like a dream.

Inside the church's large front room, the energy made me nervous. People smiled *hard*. They never broke eye contact. Friendly and unnervingly confident young men only two or three years older than myself shook my hand or hugged me in a fatherly way. Everyone was white, pale white, benevolent white, and the young people wore T-shirts and jeans as if to prove that they were here for Jesus only. Old guard church clothes were for the non-reborn.

A minute later, my sister appeared from a side room looking like a person I didn't know anymore. She worked at the church as a youth counselor now and beamed as she gave us all hugs. After pulling back, I searched her face for some hint of authenticity.

She was nice. She was so nice.

My father said something self-deprecating about his tie and she laughed then. I was relieved that it was the same high-pitched too-loud laugh that she'd always had, the laugh that was so endearing as to make strangers turn and smile. More people entered and music started playing from the sanctuary. I didn't know what to do with my hands. She had things to take care of and so she thanked us again for coming and wrapped her fingers around my forearm and squeezed. That squeeze felt like a secret. And then she walked away.

She is always walking away.

Inside the sanctuary, there were possibly two hundred people already seated. The front section of the church was built like a concert venue with multiple tapered sections of pews and a large stage set decorated with elaborate curtains. I looked up and noted the mounted speakers and professional overhead lights.

My mother led the way past the crowds and down the aisle, striding faster than usual and smiling at unfamiliar faces. "I'm not going any further," my father announced. We'd only reached the third to last row. This, apparently, was close enough.

I don't remember much of the service other than it was loud. Standing in front of amps and musical equipment, the pastor spoke in impassioned tones, his voice rising and falling. There was talk of sin and hell and redemption; his pauses were dramatic. My sister was a member of the choir that wasn't called the choir—they were introduced as the worship team. When she took the stage with the rest of the musicians and stood behind her microphone stand, my parents sat up straighter in order to see her better. Their eyes never wavered. I wished she could understand how profound their love for her is. She is their first-born; she is their miracle. But she was becoming immune to them, to me, to my perception of the world.

The music was contemporary. Onstage, young men played guitar, bass, drums, and keyboard. Everyone rose. Immediately, it was clear that the congregation was hearing something I wasn't: lifting their arms in the air and throwing their heads back, people wept through closed eyes, and I gripped the pew in front of me, watching my sister through the crowd, swaying as she sang.

Halfway through the first song, she raised her arms too—an action that reminded me of how, as children, we used to stand in a doorway and press our hands against the frame as hard as we could for at least thirty seconds. Releasing that hold triggered muscle contractions and our arms floated upward in an involuntarily motion, as if we were unfurling wings.

People moaned. They yelled and whispered *amen*, their faces lit with emotion, and I stared at her, wishing she'd glance up, wink at me, signal that this was all fine. *Look at me.* My teleported demand was selfish, but I wanted to grab her hand and lead her outside, away from this place with the sickly sweet people. I'd never led before; I am the younger sister. But I could do it now. I'd persuade her to drive up north with me to the water where we would battle black flies with bug spray and swats of our hand, push a canoe into the water and sneak up on the loons until we got too close for their comfort.

*Boom, bum-bum-bum, boom.* At night we'd sit by a campfire listening to their calls and she'd laugh and tell me that she's not okay, but she will be. And so will I.

But none of that happened. After that service at my sister's church, we repeated our earlier interactions as if now stuck in reverse. She found us in the crowd, my father made a joke, she hugged us, smiled at me, squeezed my arm, and disappeared.

Still, I declare this one more time for the worshippers in the back: despite everything that happened, I refuse to believe that it was easy for my sister to leave me.

OCCASIONALLY, I NEED soft background sound when I'm writing. I didn't grow up as an only child; I'm used to the comfort of familiar noise. That, and the quiet can feel intimidating, almost hostile, during periods of unproductivity. It highlights the absence of computer keys *clicking* or my pen scribbling.

If I choose the wrong type of noise though, it can further foil my success. Anything with lyrics, a heavy beat, or a strong melody is out. Classical music influences my emotions too much. Jazz mocks me with its cleverness and artistry. So, on my laptop I play recordings that were created with the purpose of being half-listened to, such as the white noise of rain, the crackle of fire, the *shi-shi* of ocean waves, or the distant yodeling and wailing of loons.

Once, while searching for videos of loons on YouTube, I found a video called "Sounds of Earth Loons." Due to the missing punctuation, I misread the title. I thought the recording's creator was insinuating that loons inhabit earth, yes, but originate from some other heavenly realm.

*Corny,* I thought, *but whatever.* I liked the idea of loons as feathered apparitions wailing endlessly across expansive lakes.

Days later while writing and listening to the same video, it occurred to me that "Sounds of Earth" referred to the name of the video series. This video, "Loons," was one episode of the project—its creator had just neglected to use a colon or dash. I laughed at myself, maybe harder than the misunderstanding deserved, but I was surprised at how quickly I made this jump to loons being angels, instead of birds communicating through long sliding whistles.

To allow a loon call to stimulate the ends of your nerves, to let it lull you into the safety of what must be eternity and cause you to feel celestial despite that tiny pulse of blood in your neck reminding you of your body: this *must be* a misinterpretation of the true nature of that sound. Yet, the emotion it stirs isn't invalid.

Right?

The swell of religious choral music and lowest tones of hymns still cause my throat to tighten. Despite the words, I am emotionally moved. I sometimes close my eyes and pretend that I'm my sister, although I'm careful not to sway forward enough that my feet lose the solidity of the shore.

I don't know. Maybe I am just fighting God.

A MEMORY: ALL the children are wearing matching black-and-white striped T-shirts our mothers made while we dance to the song "Jailhouse Rock" by Elvis Presley. It's a show for the elders. Lined up at the front of the main gathering room in the Methodist church in Minnesota, we're twisting to the beat.

*Boom, bum-bum-bum, boom.*

My sister dances the best; all the other kids watch and mimic her steps, including me. My parents sit up straighter to see her better. Their eyes never waver.

Later, after changing out of our church clothes, we'll walk to the edge of the water, and I'll ask her again how to whistle. Her curly hair keeps blowing into her eyes. A hound dog's distant bay is carried in the wind. I remember that high clean sound of water-plucked pebbles tumbling inside the pockets of my windbreaker. And she'll tell me that I already know; she'll tell me that I just have to listen.

So, I'll close my eyes, ready my mouth, and try again.

COMMUNAL

In an essay by Deborah Kapchan in the anthology *Keywords in Sound*, Kapchan describes attending a summer sanctuary for the largest Sufi order in Morocco—the Qadirriyya Boutshishiyya. During the ceremony, women sat on the floor in a circle, singing Sufi praise poems. Their eyes were closed. Strands of prayer beads ran through their fingers. As they became more swept up in the music, the women started to react. Their bodies would "jerk, swoon, scream, and sway in unpredictable ways." One woman began weeping; another jumped up yelling "Allah!" These outbursts of emotion continued throughout the ceremony.

What Kapchan witnessed is often referred to as "al-hal" or "the state," which is a transition from normal everyday states to a spiritual state. It's not unique to this group. Evangelical Christians, for instance, refer to this shift as "being possessed by the Holy Spirit." And although religious rituals use many practices to help worshippers transcend their physicality, sound is arguably the most important cog in the ceremonial wheel, as well as what helps initiate newcomers in the first place.

Given that hearing is a biological act—a flesh and bones act—the idea of using this sense to achieve "the state" is intriguing. Sound waves travel into the ear canal. The eardrum moves the vibrations through the middle ear bones into the inner ear. The brain interprets the sound and identifies it (or creates a rundown of its possible sources). But attend any religious or spiritual service and you'll notice the mysterious link between shared beliefs and music or chanting. The body is forgotten.

In another essay from *Keywords in Sound*, Jonathan Sterne considers the differences between seeing and hearing in the context of Christian spiritualism. After studying the work of twentieth-century Toronto-based spiritualist thinkers like Walter Ong, Sterne concludes that the differences between sight and hearing include the following:

Hearing immerses its subject, vision offers a perspective

Sounds come to us, but vision travels to its object

Hearing places you inside an event, seeing gives you a perspective on the event

Hearing tends toward subjectivity, vision tends toward objectivity

Hearing is about affect, vision is about intellect

Sterne also notes that the "hallmarks of the modern era," including reason, rationalism, the subject/object split, science and capitalism, "all emerged from the privilege of sight over audition." So, whatever elements combine to create that unknowable element of faith, the link between sound and worship remains strong. In fact, even if the sound can only be heard internally ("Listen for the word of God being spoken in your heart," Christians say), it may be a requirement. After all, while the phrase "seeing is believing" was recorded as early as the mid-1600s, long before that, Jesus told his doubting disciple, Thomas, that it was more blessed to believe without seeing (John 20:29).

*Part*
*Two*

# The Sound of Undoing

These facts remain static: I lived in the outer perimeter of Boston and commuted downtown to work and graduate school. I had two roommates—two young men—who lived on the floor below me. My old dog was still alive then, although he was already losing his eyesight and hearing. I dated, occasionally.

What shifted was the heavy door that led outside to my apartment's small porch. Let's go there now. *Listen.* The door is closing from the inside. The thud of a man's shoes on the stairs backing up into the hallway heels first is growing louder. He's walking in reverse, entering my bedroom with his back toward me and rewinding into standing position with his palm on the door handle. My bedroom door shuts. Now he's rushing to take off his sweater. His face is momentarily hidden.

Pause here, as if to toggle the buttons on a remote:

Sweater on / sweater off. Sweater on / sweater off.

The stifled noise of a video game rises through the ceiling and into the attic. Both of my roommates use gaming consoles that they've plugged into their televisions so they can play against each other from the comfort of their own beds. They're laughing and yelling into their headsets; they're consumed with blasts and gunshots and the groans of fake death.

(If we were doing, not undoing, they'd tell me later that they didn't hear a thing.)

Now this man I just met tonight is taking off his shoes, followed by his jeans. Play it again: the vibrating *z-zzz* of the zipper, up and down. At the same time, my old dog is outside my closed door, confused, pacing the hallway hind legs first. His nails tap against the hardwood floor. He whines and grunts before thumping back down onto his orthopedic bed in the living room.

It's all just beginning.

TELL ME, WHAT is the sound of taking back the can't-take-back? What is the sound of erasing what has been done? I'm still unsure, but I'd like to locate this sound, listen to and memorize every vibration of it, and describe it through words with the simplest terms possible, just like you can define silence as: ~~noise.~~

I wonder if the sound of undoing is just a recording of my life in reverse, waiting for the *click* that signals I've reached the pivotal first moment and can start anew. I like this idea of starting anew. I am, perhaps, obsessed with it. But even if I could rewind to the time before I met this man would there be some flicker of past pain remaining?

When I was young, my father spent much of his free time recording clips off the television onto videocassettes. He had dozens of tapes stacked in dresser drawers in the basement. Descriptions of the clips' contents had been scribbled on all their labels, and then, more often than not, crossed out. If he came across something he liked while flipping through the channels, he inserted a preselected tape into the VCR and fast-forwarded or rewound to clips that he didn't care to keep or at least could let go of. Then he recorded over them. In this way, the tapes were always changing.

Yet, due to the imprecision of the VCR, many of the original clips never disappeared. Instead, his tapes became video collages. A two- or three-second blurb of John Wayne riding into town on a horse would morph and bleed into Jimmy Hendrix bent over his guitar. A pack of wolves chasing prey fell away and was replaced by a polka band performing for the local public access channel. I remember watching a home video of my sister and me doing a choreographed dance in matching T-shirts—the camera was zoomed in too close and recorded us mostly from the knees down—but then the tape went low and loud in sound and transformed into a scene of Big Bird near the Great Wall, talking to a child. Why was Big Bird in China? The clip only lasted a few seconds; I didn't know.

My father sat in his recliner in the dark, hitting the record button, hitting "stop," rewinding, rewinding, rewinding, but remnants of the past clung to the outer edges of each recording, serving as a reminder that it had been there.

Serving as a reminder that it had been.

I AM STILL undoing. It is a dirty business.

From my mattress on the floor of my bedroom, I'm screaming, then I'm yelling, and words stream out of my mouth in reverse, saying, "Leave, please. Go." Now I'm just talking, just finding my voice, but I remember at the time that I didn't recognize my own intonation and tone. It sounded like when you hear yourself on a recording for the first time and go, "Is that me? Why didn't anyone tell me that I sound like that?" and then someone else in the room says, "Sound like *what*? You?"

I'd lifted my right arm and pointed toward the door while clutching a blanket to my chest. But now I'm back down, my face stuffed into my pillow, and I can't make out individual sounds. They are all rushing to meet each other as if I'm inside a blender.

When I'm awake, I'm aware of what's happening to me for a few seconds, in and out, but I'm unable to move. I can only gurgle. At least I can hear the *garomphh garomphh* of my heartbeat. When I'm not awake, it's like I'm dead. Who is to say I'm not? He did not try to determine otherwise.

WHEN MY FATHER recorded a new snippet of a show, he would shout at my sister and me from downstairs, maybe with a drink in hand, saying, "Hey girls, I've got something to show you!" And he'd wait there in his recliner with the tape rewound to just the right spot at the beginning of the clip, held there in suspense with the pause button so that he could give a little introduction before hitting play.

Afterward, he'd rewind to the start after it finished, maybe two or three more times depending on its length, so we could enjoy it again. I watched these tapes so much that, even though they transformed over the years, I could tell you what scenes were coming next in reverse with my eyes closed.

But at some point, after all those tens of dozens of clips overlapped each other, the tapes became corrupted. As my father would play a clip of Lawrence Welk conducting a band, you could see the face of Richard Pryor onstage behind him, pushing through the image, grinning. Shapes lost their form. Electric pink, blue, and yellow squiggly lines flashed across the screen. And the sound garbled—it'd become too suddenly loud and then would go quiet.

"This tape is almost a goner," my father lamented. If the tape eventually spilled its guts out inside the VCR, my sister or I would eject it, stick a finger into one of its spools and twist the magnetic tape back into the roll.

The tapes never ceased function; they were just incoherent. You no longer knew if they were playing backward or forward.

BACK, BACK, BACK. He's handing me a glass filled with vodka, no ice, even though I'd been begging for water.

I begged a man for a glass of water in my own kitchen.

I don't know where the bottle of vodka came from—it's not mine; it's not my roommates'—but the sound of liquor is very much like the sound of water, just a bit more sluggish. The clear liquid slides up against the side of the glass when agitated, creating a dumber, thicker *ooosshhh*.

Meaning, I should have known.

And yet, when even your own body falling to the floor does not cause hot waves of pain but instead results in a nice, cool feeling interrupted only by the sharp ring of atmospheric fuzz in your ears, a slow stream of vodka *ooshhhing* down your throat doesn't alert you. The choking high-proof taste of briny water does.

"Good girl," this voice you barely recognize says in reverse. You hear him taking off your dress and he's struggling to free your arms from the sleeves.

Forgive me. I am jumping around in time. It was all so confusing, even when I had no choice but to let it play.

I IMAGINE THAT the sound of undoing is muffled, bizarre, rising when it should be falling. It's the sound of too much speed—high-pitched as if amplified by helium—but when you slow it down, the sound is dark and grotesque. It's too low for your lungs. Everyone becomes a monster, if they weren't already one in the doing.

"If only life were like a blouse," I told a friend a few weeks after that man left my apartment, but I couldn't really elaborate on the simile. I knew it wasn't revolutionary. I think my point was that you could button and unbutton with just a quick twiddling of fingers and thumbs, swapping out outfits and colors and styles at a whim. Checking to see what works. Checking to see what doesn't. Checking to see what almost kills you. Checking to see what you'll wish away at night while clutching the thick white fur of your dog. A blouse is even simpler than a tape; it gets stretched out, a button comes loose, but it doesn't corrupt and sputter.

The problem, of course, is that with all that freedom to undo, we'd no longer be who we are because—as I've been told—who we are is what we do.

Or is it what has been done unto us?

LET ME UNDO further, undo faster. Do you know what a recording of the inside of an overcrowded bar on a Friday night played in reverse sounds like? It sounds like an overcrowded bar. Music streamed backward still has a beat, still competes for your sacred ear space against the noise of boisterous young people, primarily college students, who are talking too intensely—they're shouting and cackling—and their chairs squeak across the tiled floor when they walk backward from the door and sit down. Sweaty pint glasses *thump* against the wooden tables after they pull the beer away from their mouths.

And in this place, this man, my date, is sitting next to me on a barstool. There's the *clink* of the third tequila shot, then the second, then the first. He is about to start ordering them. *Buck up*, I tell myself when the bartender smirks at him, barely looks at me, and pushes a dish of salt and two lime wedges toward us. This is a game between both men; I should have known that I could not win.

Rewind, rewind, listen to the warped laughter dying down as he closes the bar's door from the outside. We're both backing out. Our movements are sporadic and twitchy in reverse.

Now we're on the street conversing, giving each other a quick hug as a greeting and he's walking backward away from me. I'm standing on the sidewalk near the corner of Beacon Street and Strathmore Road, and the cars are reversing at high speed. The *whoosh* of traffic stresses my body and makes me feel trapped. I uncross my arms. From twenty feet away I knew I didn't like him but here I am, acting polite, smiling. He's heavier than in the pictures, perhaps by forty pounds, which wouldn't bother me if it weren't for the fact that his beard is also gone and he's no longer wearing glasses. His photos—the tiny proof of personhood we'd shared with each other online—were riddled with lies.

We had planned on meeting in the North End for dinner instead of here, a few blocks from my apartment. But an hour before the agreed upon time, he texted and asked to meet me on this corner instead because he was already in the neighborhood and he was carrying a heavy camera bag. Could he drop it off at my apartment first and then maybe we could just go to a bar nearby? He doesn't want his expensive camera stolen or broken.

I skipped this part earlier while rewinding—closed my eyes and hummed as it came into view. He already had me sunk before I even took a sip of a drink; he had an excuse to come back to my apartment. When had I learned how to trust? If I could only record over just five minutes of time, these might be the five I choose.

SPEAKING OF MINUTES, if we could undo, would we lose gaps of time? Minutes, hours, maybe days of time? Could I create a new memory—a new reality—in this reality's place? The sound of undoing is strange, but I suppose it's the redoing that I'm concerned about. The process may be messy or fall apart as soon as I start. If I have learned anything from my father's tapes, it's that the past will seep into the present, no matter how many times you try to rewrite.

In fact, the process will worsen the more you try.

Yet, it has been six years and I cannot let go. It keeps me awake or makes me cringe and pour another glass of wine. I focus on the sounds of the past—the *creak* of the door, the deep voice of the bartender—instead of existing in the present.

Thus, despite the risk that the pain will resurface and echo inside my head, I wish for a blank point to restart from. I don't know what I'll fill this space with exactly, but I know that I'll record a new night. One where I text my date an excuse for why I must cancel—no apology—and perhaps go out for a slow walk with the dog instead or read a book in the chair nearest the north-facing window. I'll boil water for tea and call a friend. I'll head into the city like I was supposed to.

Of course, I'll have to keep recording over everything that follows—tapes and tapes of time that showed me breaking down at the doctor's office, curling up in the corners of my bedroom, tracing my fingers along the walls, sleeping for hours, then days, without end.

In this new version of events, I won't find a subletter for my room in the apartment and move out without giving my roommates a reason. I won't sleep on a friend's couch, and then in another man's bed, and lose all interest in books and writing and food.

But I also won't be angry. I won't scream at the wind when it knocks me off my feet down by the harbor, forcing me to reconcile with how much I've changed (or is it how much I've lost?) or the fact that I'm ready now to start fighting for my life. I won't rise to my feet and use a dirty tissue I find stuffed in my coat pocket to clean the blood off my knees and, with tears on my face, think, *this is the most alive I've ever felt.*

No, forget all that. Instead, I'll live a new life, possibly corrupted by the sound of one already lived. Or maybe not.

HERE I AM at the sound of my footsteps, soft taps in black flats against the sidewalk, leading back up the wooden outdoor stairs, my keys jingling as they reverse out of a small pocket inside my purse. My jaw lets off a bright, surprising *pop* as my hand grasps the handle of the door. My joints do this when I'm tense; my nervousness is audible.

The electric wires that dangle just above the chain link fence in the back of my apartment building are crackling. Vibrating. I can hear the neighbor's pit bull sucking in its own barks from the edge of its dirt yard; it's inhaling a loud, repeated warning, back, back, back, until it's just sniffing air, its nose raised to the dusky sky, before lowering to the ground again, listening for something that may or may not be coming.

And this is where the tape *clicks.*

This is where my life goes—.

- - - - - - - - - - - - - - - - - - - - - - - - - - - - - - - - - -

### TRAUMA

In films and television, characters remembering traumatic past events often experience flashbacks in the form of images: the knife, the fiery explosion, the oncoming car, a woman clutching a limp baby, a man's twisted and angry face, their hands, his hands, blood. But trauma is also often connected to memories through sound: a scream, a "boom" or "bang," ragged breathing, a voice or voices.

In fact, the correlation between trauma and sound has been increasingly studied in the wake of U.S. and British soldiers returning home from war in Iraq and Afghanistan. For instance, in 2015, researchers at NYU Langone Medical Center found that brief exposure to sudden sounds connected to mild trauma can form long-term memories in the locus coeruleus—a region of the brain associated with physiological responses to stress and panic.

In one set of the experiments, the investigators paired a specific sound with a series of mild shocks delivered to a group of poor rats. As long as the sound continued to play, the activity in the rats' brains spiked, even after the shocks stopped.

A.k.a. the sound played / the rats' bodies clenched in fear.

Furthermore, in 2018, researchers at the University of Cambridge studied the link between post-traumatic stress disorder (PTSD) and auditory hallucinations. The subjects included military veterans, as well as survivors of civilian trauma, physical trauma, and sexual trauma. Although it's inherently difficult to study hallucinations of any kind, a small number of participants were "hearing voices that weren't really there."

The hope is that research like this can be used to lessen or reshape the symptoms of PTSD for veterans and other survivors. Now that noise, both as a trigger and as a manifestation of symptoms, is scientifically linked to "shell shock," perhaps those in need of treatment will eventually have access to more effective therapies—including, ironically, sound and music therapy.

# The Sound of Nothing

The drive from Milwaukee to the Twin Cities takes around five hours when the weather is decent, but by the time I neared the Minnesota border on a Friday afternoon in mid-November, rain heaved across the interstate. I'd felt so nervous about arriving late that I pulled into the parking lot of Orfield Labs—a commercial sound lab on the industrial southeast side of Minneapolis—over a half hour before my reserved private tour and killed the engine. Through my rearview mirror, I studied the lab's indistinctive exterior. Inside, there was a room that the Guinness World Records deemed the "quietest place on earth," but without GPS, I would have driven right past the featureless, vine-smothered cement building.

Rain no longer smacked against my windshield, but it was too cold to wait in the car. I grabbed my satchel and shuffled toward the sound lab's entrance. In a city park across the street, a few preteen boys in puffy coats gathered underneath the steel-hued sky. Despite the hum of interstate traffic from four blocks away, their laughter was audible, triggering a memory: kids grouped together like that in a park near my parents' house on the east side of Iowa City. The park was cut in half by a street, underneath which ran two parallel cement tunnels. If the creek flooded, they became an overflow route. My older sister and I used to race through the graffiti-filled tubes, the rumble of cars over our heads, our tennis shoes getting soggy in the muck.

It was my favorite game, until one day she didn't come out the other side.

Shuddering in the damp air, I listened to the kids for a moment more before opening the sound lab's door. Their voices faded, a rush of heated air hit my face, and a woman behind the front desk directed me to a couch where I could wait.

Too anxious to sit, I jotted down observations in my journal. The front room was cluttered with unsheathed vinyl records, wooden clocks, and clippings of news stories written about Orfield Labs. Almost a dozen framed album covers also hung on the wall. The building originally functioned as Sound80, a recording studio founded in 1969, and had been used by a diverse range of musicians, including Minnesota native Prince. *Blood on the Tracks* by Bob Dylan and *Izitso* by Cat Stevens had also both been recorded here. But the label sold the building in 1990 to Steve Orfield, an acoustics and sound researcher.

Eventually two older men—one with a thick beard, one with a long silver ponytail, both hippie throwbacks and longtime employees—appeared from another room. After introductions, the man with the beard crossed his arms and asked me why I'd booked a tour. Warmth rising in my cheeks, I told them I was curious about noise and hearing, that I wanted to write a story on the lab and its silent chamber. They nodded and signaled for me to follow them toward the first studio. I exhaled in relief. I'd dreaded the inevitable question, as there was more to the answer.

During the past few years, I'd noticed that sound seemed to be the connecting force between my past and present. Everyday noises snapped me back into moments from childhood. I heard kids laughing and thought of my sister. Thunder rumbled and I was once again a teenager alone in the woods, scrambling to get home before a storm let loose. A chair dragged across a wooden floor, and I remembered nothing—but, for a moment, my body pulsed with nausea. Voices came to me in waves, as muffled as they'd be underwater, but I couldn't flesh out any other senses enough to solidify memories.

As I walked through the sound lab, I wondered if silence could unlock some insight about the past, or allow me to tap into an inner, hidden layer of my being. At the age of thirty-one, I felt like there were holes where blocks of time should have been. Maybe a visit to this room would allow me the clarity to retrace memories—memories, I sensed, that were somehow related to my sister. If I stripped away all the noise, would it finally be quiet enough for me to remember what had occurred?

The first room the two men showed me was an old recording studio where producers and musicians had played back tracks. The booth still functioned, but now the low-lit room was crammed with consumer goods, microphones, and machines instead of instruments. Corporations hired the lab to evaluate and adjust the sound of their products. New vacuum cleaner models can't be too quiet, for instance, or else users will subconsciously perceive them as being less efficient. Motorcycles pose a similar problem. European markets require lower decibel levels but, according to the manufacturers, if you drastically change the *roar* of an engine, you take away the nostalgia and feeling of power elicited in the rider. Architectural firms pay the lab to test designs and materials as well. I fiddled with a few of their experiments and imagined living in a house with sound wave–absorbing carpet. Few noises would enter and challenge my sense of peace; even my own footfalls would be dampened.

The tour continued in a whitewashed room used to measure reverberation, which was reminiscent of a school gymnasium. Door-size sheets of metal were strung from the high ceilings. I amused myself by wandering to each corner and testing the acoustics. My voice was canceled out in a few small pockets of space, and I whispered nonsensical words, trying to push them away from me and out into the air. They were deadened upon rolling over my lips. But after taking one or two steps to my right or left, a simple note I sung went pinballing around the room.

My echoing voice took me back to where it always takes me: I was eight and my sister was eleven when I ran the length of one cement tunnel and, blinking in the sunlight, waited on the steep south-facing overhang for her to emerge from the other. I heard a car passing on the street overhead, birdsong, the slow trickle of the creek, and my heartbeat in my ears. It was too quiet. I couldn't detect the *thump* of her footsteps, so I sidled over to the opening of the second tunnel, turned my head, and called her name. My voice reverberated down the empty tube and out the other side. She was gone.

Lowering my head, I stepped into the cement tube where my sister was supposed to be and ran back to the other side, pressing my outstretched arms against the curved walls for balance. When I reached the end and she wasn't there, my throat tightened. After sidestepping along the north-facing overhang, I climbed to street level. Gazing over a tree-lined field, I noticed a figure sitting cross-legged in the grass, facing away from me. I sprinted across the field, sweat beading on my back, and grabbed her shoulder. Out of breath, I asked what happened. She looked up at me, flashed a slight closed-mouth smile, and with a flat expression in her eyes, said, "Nothing."

I used that same word over twenty years later, when she called me from her home in Iowa and asked if I knew what had happened to us. Kumar was still at work, the house was quiet, and I was staring at a blank document on my laptop screen while my smallest dog snored in my lap. She told me she'd been questioning for a long time if there was something we weren't remembering. Her years of depression and anxiety refused to be alleviated by medication. She was flooded with flashbacks—memories mostly comprised of sounds and feelings. Every therapist she and I had seen said our issues resembled those of someone who'd been sexually abused as a child.

"You have the same issues as me," she said in a hushed voice. "The depression, the anxiety, the low self-esteem—haven't you even considered it?"

I could hear the muffled voices of her children in the background. The muscles in my shoulders tensed, my skin turned cold, and I clutched my dog tighter. It was before noon and the half-empty bottle of local Wisconsin beer sitting before me took on new meaning: guilt, shame, a constant need to escape. Still, I told her the truth, which was the only truth I knew: I didn't remember anything, and I was suspicious of any mental health professional I'd worked with in the past who'd questioned me about the possibility of abuse. They asked things like Was I touched? Was I assaulted? Was it ongoing or maybe just once?

*Stop poking at it*, I wanted to say to them. *There's nothing there.*

My last psychiatrist had leaned forward in her armchair and suggested, again, that we could work on remembering—it's possible that those memories are repressed, she said—and I told her no, that I've tried, but I don't want to be influenced to fill those holes with warped or invented happenings.

Since I was a child growing up in Iowa, I'd searched my brain for a sound, a hand, a face, a ceiling or floor—my mind seemed to do it automatically while I lied in bed at night. I scrolled through mental checklists, remembering my earliest interactions with men. At night, I even dreamed of walking through houses with endless rooms, peering under washing machines or opening kitchen cupboards. These houses weren't vast or old or abandoned, like they often are in horror films. They were lower-middle-class ranch homes with wood-paneled walls and dark orange carpet. The bathrooms were tiled in mint green; the windows were framed with thick polyester curtains. They were houses from the Midwest, conglomerates, likely, of family and friends' homes that I'd visited as a kid. And in these dreams, I was searching for one thing: clues that would reveal my silent, supposed, invisible abuser.

Before that phone call, I had no idea my sister was doing the same.

In Milwaukee, with the phone pressed to my ear, I took another swig of beer and told her I needed to get back to my freelance work. I could hear at least two of her children pleading for her attention but, despite the commotion, she seemed disappointed. We said bye and, like usual, didn't talk again for months.

Inside the reverberation room in Minnesota, I listened to my words deflect off the metal pieces hung round the room.

"Echo! Echo!" my voice repeated. "Can you hear me?"

"I can hear you!" the man with the silver ponytail answered. He smiled as his response bounced from wall to wall. I laughed, picked up my bag, and followed him into the hallway. Both men stood in front of a door that looked like the entrance to a meatpacking plant's industrial-size freezer.

"Are you ready to try out the anechoic chamber?" the man with the beard asked. I nodded and he wished me luck as the other man opened the massive door.

Upon entering the space, I tried to ignore the fact that I'd just followed a stranger into a room with no exits, no cell phone reception, a door that locks upon closing and from which no sound can leave or enter.

The chamber itself was 99.99 percent silent. All four walls, the ceiling, and the floor were constructed from thick chunks of cardboard-colored fiberglass, resembling accordion files. Stacked in alternating horizontal and vertical rows, the fiberglass was held together by chicken wire that had been wrapped in sound-absorbing foam. These rows of insulation were placed on top of giant springs, creating the feeling that we were inside a life-size jack-in-the-box. Outside, two thick walls of concrete, separated by a layer of air space, encased the room.

This level of sound deprivation not only earned Orfield Labs a record for being home to the quietest place in the world but also raised concerns about the reactions it might cause in its visitors. Over the years, a story had spread in the local media claiming that a person could "lose their mind" after just forty-five minutes inside the chamber. According to my tour guides, the claim was false. Still, due to safety concerns, visitors were only allotted a maximum of fifteen minutes.

As the man with the silver ponytail explained how they use the room to measure the true decibel levels of machines and other products, I relaxed and took notes. But the scratching sound of my pen was so exaggerated that it felt embarrassing, as if I were humming during a lecture. My body's sounds made me self-conscious as well. A quick sniffle of my nose was now brash enough to draw attention.

The quality of the man's voice, however, seemed normal, if only slightly compressed. It wasn't until he turned around to demonstrate how sound carries in the room that the difference became apparent. Even though he was standing three feet away, it sounded as if he'd walked the length of a city block and was now chatting with someone else. His words were only decipherable when he was aiming them straight at me.

"So, how long do you want to spend in here alone?" he asked after turning back around.

My ultimate worry was that I'd panic. I assumed that time would move slower than usual, and if fifteen minutes felt like thirty minutes or an hour, then I could start entertaining the possibility that something had gone wrong: a fire in the building, all three employees simultaneously suffering heart attacks, a conspiracy to employ me as a sensory-deprived sex slave. Still, I chose the fifteen minutes.

After he fetched a chair for me, I sat down, turned my cell phone off so as not to be tempted to peek at the time every minute, and placed my belongings at my feet.

"Lights on or off?" he asked.

"Off," I said. "Might as well get the full experience."

I stole one last glance at my surroundings, nervously smiled at him as he stood in the doorway, and took a deep breath. He left, shutting the heavy door behind him. The lights went off. The air seemed to leave the room. My body froze, as if too stunned to move.

The first thought that came to me was, *oh, shit.*

The day my sister disappeared in the park with no explanation was the first time that I experienced her disassociating from the world, or at least the world that I was living in. The experience left me feeling confused, but also angry. To have unknowingly run through that tunnel on my own felt like a betrayal. Why hadn't she told me where she was going or what she was doing? Why hadn't she taken me with her? My older sister was not only my sibling, best friend, and role model—she was also my protector.

The incident was only the beginning though. Over the years, her connection to the present time and place occasionally lapsed and I'd lose her, even if she sat across from me at the kitchen table. One moment we'd be laughing and telling stories; the next, her expression wilted, and she wandered out of the room, saying she needed to be alone. Or she stared into spaces ahead or around her, but always right through me.

On the walk back home from the park that day, she apologized for having left me at the tunnels, but it felt as if she was sorry for accidentally stepping on the back of my shoe—not for disappearing.

When she joined that deeply conservative Evangelical church, I was scared, hurt, and perplexed. But I wasn't shocked. She'd been escaping to the edges of our shared environment for a long time before someone finally offered her a chance to leave it entirely and be reborn. Maybe the new purpose helped her cope with the trauma or at least reframe it. Maybe she assumed that I didn't need her anymore, that life wouldn't be desperately quiet without her.

Inside the anechoic chamber, my heart rate immediately spiked in response to the deprivation of senses. *Breathe*, I told myself. I forced a smile and registered my facial muscles tightening to lift the corners of my lips. Moving with caution, I experimented with my lack of vision like a child: I waved my hands in front of my face and opened and closed my eyes. Opened was blackness; closed was a dark universe of ever-shifting neon colors, a cosmic array of the blood vessels on the inside of my eyelids.

Next, I began to test the sound in the chamber. I rubbed my fingertips together, snapped a few times, whacked my pen against my leg, whispered. These micro acts were louder due to the lack of interference, but I recognized that I was simply distracting myself to pass the time. I remembered what I'd hoped to get out of this experience and sensed the tinge of a headache rooting itself in the back of my head.

After I forced myself to sit still and concentrate, my response to the sensory deprivation quickly changed. My eyes felt unprotected. Soon, I struggled to keep them open, not out of fatigue, but out of fear. It became even more difficult to sit up straight with my head held high. My body wanted to tuck my chin into my chest, wrap my arms around my torso, and sink down into the chair. How easy it would have been to become a goblin in that cave, to back into a corner and bury my face into my knees.

I had hoped that silence might give me the aural space and clarity to remember what had happened, or to decide, once and for all, that nothing had happened. It would be peaceful, like a final letting go of whatever had been repressed inside me for all these years. Yet the total lack of sound, more than my loss of sight, made me feel deeply vulnerable. In its absence for the first time ever, I realized that sound is a protective blanket, as all-encompassing as amniotic fluid. A slight wind in the trees, the coo of mourning doves, the crunch of fallen leaves, the *shi-shi* of ocean waves—all these sounds envelop me and keep me safe from a stark world. They remind me that I'm alive, that I'm not alone.

For those who have always lived with sound, silence is oppressive.

Unnerved, I regretted my choice to come until I discerned something else: the sound of the pulsing blood in my neck. The noise was as quiet as a moth landing on a windowsill. But I could hear that slight, rhythmic *whoosh* of liquid in my veins. As my aural perception expanded, I also listened to the wet noise of my throat swallowing saliva, the gurgle of my belly, and my breath moving in and out of my lungs.

Among this internal-body background noise, I started to debate what silence really is. Beyond the blood, saliva, acid, and oxygen, my inner voice also became so disruptive, that, for being in a silent room, the whole experience was very loud. No, my thoughts weren't physically communicated by an airstream forced through my voice box, over my tongue, past my teeth, and out into the atmosphere. But even though only I could hear the pitch, tone, and timbre of my own voice within my head, wasn't it still sound?

I could have been sitting in a chair in the realm of zero—in a pre-explosion universe—but there would still be noise. I was the felled tree in the forest. Still, I had to somehow shut it all up at least for a few minutes. If I wanted to unlock some deeper part of me, I needed to stop my mind from making so much racket. Thus, I rested my hands lightly in my lap and stared into the space between my eyes, trying to separate myself from reality. I rested my eyelids at half-mast. By looking into the center of my perspective, within the span of one minute or maybe five minutes—I didn't know—I started to lose a sense of the space that my body occupied and then a sense of my body altogether.

Shaking the perception of my own physicality made me feel high, like I was floating just outside the constraints of my skin, but I needed a new identity. Free from sight and society, I willfully shape-shifted into a cat. I hadn't gone insane. It was just easy to alter whatever ideas I held of my physical self. Cats remain confident and stealthy in a world devoid of light and noise, so it seemed like the right choice to take on this new fearless nature. And soon after my feline transformation, I almost converted into nothing. I had been a woman sitting in a padded, windowless room, and then a cat, and then, moments later, I was on the verge of becoming a concept. Untethered from my former reality, I no longer registered ideas of myself. It was as if I had been washed clean, as if I too could become reborn.

The next thing I remember was the chamber's door opening and the lights switching on. Almost no time had passed at all.

I felt as if I'd just woken up from a dreamless nap, but I wasn't changed. No memories or insights had come to me. Nevertheless, as I adjusted back to light and sound, I had an insight: if something had been done to me, to my body, to my sister's body, I might never know, I might never remember, even if I wanted the memory to return to me so I could see it, hear it, feel it, scream at it, cry over it, beat it with abstract fists, and then throw it away forever.

The man with the ponytail appeared in the doorway, asking how I was. "Great," I said, but I couldn't find my balance upon standing and braced myself against the chair. While leaving the room, I thanked both men for the tour and walked outside into the gray light, ducking as if I might hit my head on the sky. After startling at the sound of a vehicle alarm, I got back in my car and drove away.

That night, while sitting on the bed in my hotel room in downtown Minneapolis, I opened my laptop and attempted to analyze my experience. I wanted to conclude something. Anything. And in the absence of a personal epiphany, I pondered whether, even in the quietest place on earth, was I able to experience true silence? Are we able to experience the sound of nothing?

*Merriam-Webster* defines "nothing" as: "Not any thing. No thing. No part." And if nothing is "no thing" then, of course, one can assume that nothing also makes no noise. How would I describe the absence of sound waves and vibrations through the flat, flawed, invented medium of the English language? How could I put the sound of nothing into words? The task felt like trying to define the universe through, say, clay. Tangible materials felt insufficient in the face of the incomprehensible.

If all I had to work with was wet brown earth, though, I'd take some of it in my hands, rip off various-size pieces and roll them into little balls. Those spheres would represent the planets, moon, stars, and sun. Afterward, I'd dry them, hang them from the ceiling with string and meander around them, making sure to linger in the empty spaces like a speck of dust, like a witness.

That's how limited my mind is: I'm only able to define nothingness when it was juxtaposed against something-ness. Frustrated, I closed my laptop and felt that chronic, trembling need to tamp down the rising bad feelings and fast. Alcohol, my escape, is always fast. I pulled on my coat and went out for a drink.

It was the following early spring when my sister phoned and shared something that was glimmering in what had previously been an empty space for her. She hadn't wanted to burden me with it earlier, but she recalled a series of memories from an in-home daycare in Minnesota where we used to be dropped off on weekdays. This was before we moved to Iowa, before I would have been old enough to start preschool. The memories involved her; they involved me. She remembered me screaming and crying when they took me upstairs, still shrieking when I was a floor above her, and there she was, laid out on a twin bed, unable to do anything to save herself or her younger sister.

"There was more than one man," she said. "It wasn't just the adult son."

My limbs shook after we hung up the phone. Now, there was a story. Now, there were the sounds of fear. Now there was a man, or men. Still, I did not trust that I could only *feel* the truth—like if I leaned forward in my chair enough, I could just fall into it, right through the floor, instead of *know* it, like really know it, so I could measure it, study it, and record it once and for all.

I understood the critical importance of believing a story of abuse told by another person, by another woman, by my sister. I listened, told her how sorry I was, told her that I loved her, promised her not to question or mention it to our parents until she was ready. She could call me whenever or I could meet her wherever. I could drive down to Iowa and take her to the hospital if her depression worsened. But that night, all I could think about was whether nothing is still nothing if it pulses with the sound of someone else's memories.

Over the following weeks, I retreated from my efforts to identify any past clues. I couldn't uncover any memory that might have confirmed the abuse. My sister didn't call again. *Enough*, I said, and opened beer after beer. Months passed and I started to refuse myself the alcohol and tried meditation and exercise instead. With patience and perseverance, walking my dogs, going for a run, or merely sitting and closing my eyes triggered a similar release. Inside the 120-year-old house in Milwaukee I shared with my husband, I closed my eyes and could hear the twittering of sparrows and the raucous call of seagulls, a nearing police siren, a car screeching its tires during a too-fast turn onto Center Street, and a breeze blowing off Lake Michigan, rattling my neighbor's unhinged screen door. I liked sitting on my back porch with my legs stretched out on the wooden planks, listening to my two dogs rubbing their backs against the grass or growling at the footsteps of a man walking through the alleyway.

In late June, my husband and I drove to southeastern Ohio with our dogs and stayed in a log cabin in the Hocking Hills, just north of the Appalachian Mountains. Due to the humidity and density of trees, the sound felt dampened there, minus the noise of frogs croaking into the early morning hours. Mist settled over the tops of the dark green hills in the mornings and didn't dissipate until the evenings. And the state park was filled with dozens of glacial-carved sandstone caves, formed over ten thousand years ago when immense lobes of ice retreated north toward Wisconsin.

The largest, most impressive caves were crowded with slow-moving tourists and panting dogs straining against their leashes, but the smaller ones—the ones that require hours of hiking along slick, rocky trails—remained devoid of other people. Upon arriving at the opening of a recess cave tucked into a small cliff, my husband wandered toward a stream to scramble up a boulder and rest. My smallest dog paused near my feet, wagging her curly tail.

As I stood at the lip of the cave, I wondered if I'd uncovered as much truth as I ever would. I used to imagine truth as this whole, round, unblemished thing—like a pebble plucked from the water. But when muddled by the inevitable limitations of existence, it becomes slippery, shapeless, and riddled with holes. Inside the anechoic chamber at Orfield Labs, I'd witnessed the evidence of my living, fragile flesh: the *pop* of a joint as I turned my neck, the small *whiffs* of air entering and exiting my nostrils. Which was to say that I could pay to sit in a hushed, pitch-black room and—while deprived of my normal sense of perception of my body, my surroundings, my understanding of the world and time—I did not hear pure, perfect silence. I did not hear nothing. I had only experienced the closest thing to it, in the context of my beating heart.

The wind picked up for a moment, whistling as it moved through the rock formations, and I yelled, "Hello?" into the depths of the cave. My voice echoed back toward my body, asking for confirmation: Was anybody there? I shook my head, felt tears coming to my eyes, and swallowed, hard. My dog, in all her sweetness, pressed her velvety ears back against her head and looked up at me. I turned and followed her away from the pit in the earth and back out into the soundscape, her unhooked leash and collar jingling in my hand, my husband and other dog waiting for us near the chiming water, my mind, for just a moment, quiet.

In 1953, two researchers from the Audiology Clinic in New York City, Morris F. Heller and Moe Bergman, placed eighty people in a soundproof room for five minutes each. During that time, nearly all their subjects, including both hearing and deaf people, reported "hearing things." They described this phenomenon as non-vibratory tinnitus, or "an illusion of sound caused by an irritation of the auditory neural elements."

While tinnitus, a chronic high-pitched ringing sound, is often linked to noise-induced hearing loss caused by damage to the cochlea (or inner ear), Heller and Bergman were the first to discover that tinnitus can also be the ear's natural response to the sound of nothing. Now, the question of whether deaf people hear "nothing," "an inner voice," or something different altogether regularly pops up on social discussion sites, such as Quora or Reddit. Hearing people wish to understand how deaf people experience life; deaf people patiently respond to these queries, which are sometimes offensive in nature.

The answers vary, usually depending on whether people are partially deaf, were born deaf, or lost their hearing later on in life. Some responders report that they experience tinnitus. Others hear a static sound. Most deaf people explain that they "hear" in sign language though—as in, they envision their hands moving. (Or, depending on the person, they may instead visualize a pair of lips forming words.) Many deaf people "hear" in mental shapes, movements, and/or images, as well.

Whatever an individual's personal experiences may be, more recent studies have also shown that deaf people are notably better at processing peripheral vision and motion. In fact, it's possible that deaf individuals use several brain regions, particularly auditory ones, to process vision. Research also suggests that individuals who were born deaf use their audio cortex (the "hearing" part of their brain) to process both touch and visual stimuli more than hearing people.

All of this is to state the obvious: deaf people aren't lacking one of their perceptive senses. Rather, they just have different—or, yes, even enhanced—physiological capacities than hearing people. Moreover, whether you hear in the traditional sense or in another way, it's clear that our bodies will always fill a "silent" space with sound, whether it can be labeled as sound by an outsider's ears or not.

# The Sound of an Imitated Ocean

*Imitation 1*

If I sat you in a dark room, placed my open palms on the surface of an unfolded bath towel, and ran them up and down the fabric like I'm stretching bread dough, you'd identify the breaking of waves, the organic rhythm of the static-filled *ooooo-shhhh*, and say it sounds like the ocean. Like foamy salt water thinning out on the sand before retreating, the fixed vowel—the *ooooo-shhhh*—even tapers in volume as I slide my hands back across the towel toward my body.

I know this because I've heard it before.

First, I draped the towel over my kitchen table. I moved a chair aside and stood there with my eyes closed, trying not to think. The house was empty; the only noise was the refrigerator, which was barely humming. *But still*, I thought. *Humming*. Yet it was quiet enough that running my palms against the towel became almost involuntary, as if I wasn't doing it; my breath was doing it.

Eventually my breath became the water, exhaling waves, inhaling them back in, though I realized there was a time in my life when this action would have seemed like invisible fingers from the dry earth—the dirt, the streets, the buildings—were pulling the water in, then pushing it back out. (Like the ocean, in all her power, was being acted upon, not acting.) The comparison is complicated by the moon's command over the tides, although, of course, perception is everything: I suspect that the moon no more commands the ocean than a woman commands her ovaries.

After fifteen minutes or so, my palms began to feel burnt and thus the soothing aural effect dissipated. I refolded the towel. Later, I used it to dry off after taking a shower. A towel is just a towel, until it isn't.

*Imitation 2*

When I was twenty-three years old, a man who was a friend of my roommate's took me to a strip club in Denver, Colorado. I remember: alleyway, blinking red lights, grim-faced bouncers checking IDs at the door, another young woman—his ex-girlfriend and later his ex-wife—smiling at me as if to ask, "Isn't this great?" I had just moved to town and the man took an interest in me, though I would have been wise to avoid him; the other woman only acted genial with me when men were about, as if our silly, almost flirtatious interactions were for the benefit of male gazes only.

Inside the club, the music, which had been a low, dull beat on the other side of the heavy door, ratcheted up enough to *thump* inside my ribs. The decor was fake gold, dark hallways, and mirrored walls. After the man exchanged two $100 bills at the front desk, he handed both me and the other young woman a thick stack of ones. The bills were so clean and crisp that I almost expected them to be warm.

"I've never seen so much cash in my life," I mumbled. The music was too loud for anyone to hear me. A bouncer held open a black velvet curtain and, with money in hand, I followed my two companions to the interior.

I'd traveled the world and seen the seedy, sometimes dangerous businesses that drive the night economy. But this was my first time walking into this type of space as a participant. For once, I felt like I was in on the game. I felt like the cool girl, free of complaints or concerns. Still, the club was less busy than I expected. Roughly twenty men—many of whom appeared to have come alone—lingered around three round tables, watching the women perform in stringy thongs and stilettos. After ordering vodka tonics, the young woman and I moved to the center of the room while the man hung back in the dark near the bar. He was here, I realized, not just to watch the dancers, but also to watch us.

There were six or seven men sitting at the table we chose. Upon locking eyes with an older man across from me, I pushed my shoulders back against my black pleather chair, lifted my chin, and adopted a cold gaze. I felt the need to take up space, to create authority, to separate myself from the women who were here to work.

The dancer on the table had long straight hair, small breasts, and a stomach that reminded me of a marathon runner's: her skin pulled taut over her abs, exposing two rows of muscle. As she danced, her eyes focused on the unlit, empty spaces of the room. When a few men started to shift in their seats and glance toward the other tables, she bent over, dropped to her knees, and then rolled onto her back. Lifting her legs high into the air, she smacked her clear six-inch plastic heels together. The noise felt like a slap, and the men whistled in response to the small act of violence.

Later, the woman kneeled in front of me, glaring. I leaned forward to tuck a dollar bill underneath one of the strings of her underwear. My fingertips grazed a bony hip. The men watched this and nodded, impressed, perhaps, with my ability to mimic them.

"Isn't she beautiful?" the young woman asked me, pointing toward the dancer's face. "I would totally fuck her." I chugged the rest of my drink, responded with something like, "Yeah, totally," but felt the dancer's eyes on me. I wondered if she'd overheard us, despite the loud music. My cheeks warmed. I pressed my lips to the rim of my glass and tilted it all the way back, even though all that remained was ice.

### Imitation 3

The day I imitated the ocean with a towel, I'd woken up in Milwaukee thinking about my former roommate in Denver. I hadn't seen her since I moved to Boston eight years earlier, which was the next city in a long line of places I failed to settle down in. Still, I had this memory of the way she would sit cross-legged on the floor in front of the television, folding her clean laundry. I'd be lounging on the couch, smoking weed and talking, but when she pressed her palms against a sweater or ran a thumb over the edge of a towel, I'd shut up and listen. The sound created by her hands against the fabric reminded me of water.

At the time, I thought I was just high. But the sound transported me out of our little downtown house with the bars on the windows and the unhoused men sleeping in the alley outside our walls to somewhere much safer, somewhere vast and open.

In Milwaukee, with that remembered feeling tickling my skin, I searched for "ocean sounds" on the internet. This produced millions of results, the top ones being recordings of waves created for the purpose of relaxation or background noise. Not knowing exactly what I was looking for, I added the term "fabric" to the search.

After scrolling through several pages of links, a video caught my attention. It was a recording of an art installation by a Turkish sound artist, Cevdet Erek. The piece, entitled "Shore Scene Soundtrack," earned him the prestigious Nam June Paik Award in 2012. As Erek noted in an interview, the installation commented not only on nature and technology but also on imitation and mimicry.

In the video, a shirtless man in a dark studio is seen running his hands over a small rectangular carpet, almost as if he's sweeping or massaging it. Microphones placed next to the carpet magnify the act, creating sounds nearly identical to ocean waves. The installation also included a manual Erek wrote called "Themes and Variations for Carpet." Like a booklet of sheet music, it provided instructions and illustrations of specific hand movements that can be used to mimic the sea.

Some art gallery visitors present at the installation likely understood this idea of mimicking and rubbed their hands against the carpet, noticed the similarities in sound between the friction of water and sand and the friction of skin and fabric, and moved on to the next displayed work. Others, perhaps, were more diligent. Maybe they let their hands wash over the carpet, thus creating a reproduction of the sound of waves, yes, but also experiencing something deeper, something closer to what it means that we can imitate this massive, powerful entity with such simplicity.

Since my husband was out for a walk with our two dogs, I decided to re-create the experience. I grabbed a bathroom towel since I didn't have a piece of carpet. Afterward, I couldn't decipher whether the act was significant in some way or as shallow as salt water that has pooled in a sunken place in the sand. I wasn't fooling anyone; the act was a meager representation of the real thing. But perhaps that was the point: I elicited the *feeling* of the ocean not by imitating the precise sound of it but by imitating something closer to the truth of its nature.

### Imitation 4

After the first dancer at the strip club finished her set, there was a lull in the action. I retreated to the table near the bar where the man still sat and handed him the remaining cash.

"I think I'm done," I told him.

"Keep it," he said. He smiled as he pushed the money back toward me. "There will be other girls you like."

He got up to order another round of drinks, leaving his half-finished glass of whiskey on the table. After a glance over my shoulder, I stole a gulp of the undiluted liquid. I couldn't figure out how to feel, but I knew I no longer wanted to be anywhere near sober.

As another topless dancer sauntered up the steps to the mini arena on the round table, I watched the young woman I'd come with cheer and scan her eyes up and down the woman's soft belly and thighs. For her, throwing money at the strippers and imitating the behaviors of men was a brash display of women's sexual liberation, or at least disguised as such. She had momentarily escaped the confines of our gender, and I could too. I just had to stop overthinking it.

Later, as the music continued to beat within my bones and the women danced, I got too drunk, laughed too loud, applauded, meandered back to the center of the room, tossed more dollar bills, and tried not to question why being here felt so intoxicating.

*If you can't beat them, join them*, I told myself while beckoning a cocktail waitress with one casually raised pointer finger. The idea was deeply misguided and riddled with weak spots, but it seemed easier than figuring out how to let myself be angry, to find strength in vulnerability, to turn on all of them and say, "No more."

*Imitation 5*

My parents drove my older sister and me to the ocean along the panhandle of Florida when I was thirteen years old. Coming from Iowa, the thin line of blue on the horizon—not corn or soybean fields, not broken with red barns or rusty silos—was bewildering. It was only my second time witnessing all that water.

Still, what I remember most from that trip aren't the waves, or the wooden piers, or the jellyfish tangled up in seaweed on the beach—their vibrancy dulled by sand and death. Instead, I remember how hyper-aware I was of my body. I was no longer just a child digging in the wet sand or wading waist deep into the cool, salty water.

Pulling at the straps and edges of my red swimsuit, I couldn't shake the external image of myself: an awkward girl, plump with baby fat, not muscular and curvy like my sister. I was envious of her flat stomach and the way her legs looked in her navy blue athletic bikini, yes, but I didn't want to look like her exactly. Instead, I wanted the multiple, emerging sources of shame to be gone: the breasts, the thickening thighs and hips, and all that flesh that remained from childhood that now seemed to be repurposing itself in specific, attention-getting places.

I'd had that rising feeling of exposure for years, but half-naked among all those beach-going strangers, I craved invisibility. I wanted to flatten my body back out and reshape it into a non-sexualized form.

As my sister and I lay on oversize towels in the sun, the breeze triggering goose bumps on our skin, I watched as skinny boys in shorts ran through the surf, pumping their arms, yelling, laughing, wrestling, mocking each other, throwing things, celebrating, doing. These thin little masculine bodies were free to move without thinking about how they were moving or about how someone else might perceive their moving. So many of them didn't have to tug at their swimsuits or monitor their appearance out of some constant, underlying fear; they didn't get watched in a way that made you wonder if someone might take something from you, or just take all of you.

That night, while listening to the rhythmic *ooooo-shhhh* of the waves from the bedroom I shared with my sister, I knew I didn't want to be a boy. But I recognized how much easier life might be if I were. Before my body even started to betray me, I'd accepted the inherent second-class status of women, the condescension and disdain with which they were treated, the objectification, the assumed weakness, the unpaid work, the thankless work, the constant fight to go *up up up* or even just *forward*. Thus, the lives of men were so alluring as to want to imitate them whenever needed.

It's no wonder then that until my early twenties, I fought back against the shifting nature of my body. The size of it felt oceanic and unruly, although all that flesh and bone didn't add up to much weight on the scale. The curved shapes and recesses of it were what I deemed dangerous. It bled, its thighs squished outward when I sat, and the breasts pushed against their too-tight keeper: the bra. From sixth grade to freshman year, I flattened my chest out most mornings by tightly wounding duct tape around my torso. I ran miles each day but still denied myself food.

At the same time that I worked to change my body, I adopted the emotional distance of men too. I could cross my arms, sniff, nod my head, and listen to any man's story with a learned seriousness. Everything that men did was important—their work, their finances, their grilling of meat, their football games. It wasn't until I was much older that I realized that this position of power isn't innate. Social norms and traditions must be learned and imitated—even violently protected—by the next generation, and the next. Without this, the structure crumbles.

On the shore that week at age thirteen, listening to the water being dragged in and then pushed out, I felt as if I was about to break open and start leaking all over the hot sand. I needed a strategy. And thus, from that point on, I acted like "one of the boys." I could also smile when asked to smile, or set tables, serve dinner, and clear plates like the other women, but mostly while in the company of men I did my best not to behave in the vexing and emotional ways that men said my gender did.

For years following, I thought I was different from all the other girls who wouldn't just go along with the patriarchal flow, who wouldn't alter or smooth out every angle of their bodies to fit the shape of the room, who expressed concerns and made demands. I made myself smaller, less conspicuous. And I embraced the raunchiness of mass male culture in the hopes that I could inherit that freedom if I just acted the part. If I just kept pretending.

In other words, I was complicit in keeping the structure standing.

*Imitation 6*

On a recent November evening, I was listening to the last raindrops of a storm drip off my roof in Milwaukee—a sound that my coffee percolator imitates in the mornings—and I thought about whether running my hands over a towel was art, like Cevdet Erek's piece. For one, the exercise was only for me, not an audience. It was also a basic physical act, as modest as my roommate folding laundry, as well as done with the purpose of testing whether I could replicate the sound of waves or, more accurately, my memory of them.

Whether art or not, it made me wonder what it means to extract essential characteristics from one entity and replicate them in the hopes of rendering it, or at least the feeling of it. Artists, of course, mimic the world around them all the time. This portrayal *can be* surface level: paintings in hotel rooms and hospitals often communicate this feeling, as if the artist only sought to create the outward appearance of a tree, a field, a cloud in the sky. In more meaningful works, an artist's interpretation may not appear as the raw object that it takes inspiration from. When we look at Joan Mitchell's paintings, we often see violence, mania, and chaos, instead of trees or sunflowers. The sculptor Ruth Asawa mimics branches and other organic and living forms with cold metal, mesh, and wires. Georgia O'Keeffe expressed the complexity and layered beauty of the American Southwest through refined and simplified brushstrokes.

Sound artist Janet Cardiff once described the sound waves in one of her installations, created by the voices of humans, as being like "ripples in the river."

Cevdet Erek made people respond to the power and persuasion of ocean waves using a piece of carpet.

If I apply this thinking about imitation to the behavior of my younger years, one conclusion I reach is this: I hadn't added anything new, or sought to portray the deepest, most toxic truths of men. Rather, I'd ingratiated myself with them through gestures, expressions, behaviors, and ways of communicating. I'd immersed myself in the study of American masculinity and only crudely mimicked its most obvious and shallow features. It's no wonder, then, that I was later left weakened and exposed, like a faint echo of the truth.

### Imitation 7

In Denver, the morning after going to the strip club, I pulled on jeans and a T-shirt and stumbled out the door in search of coffee. Weak from a hangover, my temples pounded, and my tongue felt like it'd been dipped in sand. I couldn't remember how I'd gotten home. As I turned a corner, I noticed two men sitting underneath a tree, drinking from cans concealed by paper bags. They examined me as I walked by. I raised my chin higher and tried to walk past them without feeling like I was on display. I strained to own my body and the space it took up.

"Nice ass," one of them said. The other made kissing noises.

I felt like a fool.

That day, I couldn't fill myself with anything but sleep. I'd been deeply humbled. The sex and skin from the club weren't what bothered me. I was bothered, instead, by the mile-deep division of gender: men in their chairs, women on the tables. And I had chosen the wrong side, thinking that I could pull it off.

### Imitation 8

My conduct didn't magically end after that night in Denver. This was the behavior I'd watched and mimicked for most of my formative years. To leave it behind all at once made me feel stripped of protection. I questioned who I was and what I stood for, but after squashing my doubts with alcohol or weed, all that remained was a headache. Thus, I continued to acquire straight male friends and dated men who seemed to despise me if I ever broke our unspoken agreement: I was a "cool girl," respect for my true feelings was not required. If I expressed offense or hurt, I was out.

Picking up on my laidback demeanor, men continued to talk to me as if I was one of them. They complained about their girlfriends. They stared at women as they passed by or talked about women's attributes as if they weren't people, which I knew made me not people, although I tried to differentiate myself. I felt sick to my stomach but didn't tell them to go fuck off forever. Instead, I stayed. I thought accepting the status quo demonstrated my strength, not my failings. I responded to even the most misogynistic of comments with a shake of my head and a smile, as if to say, *I don't like it, but I guess I'll tolerate it*. In reality, it felt like small parts of me were being carved out, leaving only an outer shell.

There was no final trigger that caused me to fold. Rejecting this childhood idea that strength and safety can be mined from mimicking men wasn't easy. I read books by women. I questioned myself, failed, felt disempowered, read more, and tried again. It took time to learn how to vocalize and validate how I felt. It took time to feel powerful enough as to no longer remain complicit in the objectification and oppression of women.

One night in Boston did shake me though. I was sitting in a male roommate's room surrounded by other young men, playing video games and drinking. I'd been listening, laughing along, and feigning interest for hours, but when I began telling a quick story about a robbery I witnessed near my graduate school that week, one man started talking over me as if the words coming out of my mouth weren't audible. The other men joined in. I sat there in silence, feeling emptied out. Someone eventually asked if I wanted another beer. I said no and walked away.

Surely no one noticed my absence. For me, though, the feeling of sitting in my quiet room upstairs with the door closed reminded me of the sensation that occurs when you've spent all day at the beach: that *ooooo-shhhh* of the waves is so all-consuming that when you slip free of the ocean's aural grasp and waddle back toward the road where your car is parked, the world feels too still. It's difficult for your equilibrium to adjust. Once you get in the car and try to placate the fuzz of quiet beating in your ears with the radio, the music sounds tinny and cheap. You have to turn it up, way up, in order to fill the hollow soundscape with something, anything, that can compete with the potent in and out of waves.

It took me nearly two years before I no longer felt lost and alienated. But once I figured out how to act like me—how to act with autonomy—my life started to expand with meaning.

*Imitation 9*

There is one memory from that night at the strip club that I left out earlier due to shame.

Near the end of the night, the man I came with paid for me to get a lap dance. As I followed the dancer through a hallway to a private back room, my legs unstable from the alcohol, the music shed its high notes as if it was filtered through deep water. All that was left was the vibration of bass. In a small, dim room shielded by a velvet curtain, the woman started grinding her hips over my thighs. After a few seconds, she looked at me, her eyes searching for some connection, some feeling of trust and understanding, and said, "Usually men aren't allowed to touch, but you can touch me if you want, I guess." I caught a reflection of myself in the mirrored wall. My facial expression looked calm and poised, which was confusing because, free from the influence of others' behavior, I felt small and adrift.

"No, that's okay," I said. "Just treat me the same as you would a man."

I don't remember the rest. But after the lap dance was finished, I stumbled back to the main room—the rising volume of the music guiding my way—and ordered a shot of tequila from the bar. I downed it and then ordered another.

Several years later, I looked back at this moment and thought: that was the moment when you forgot who you were and started teetering on the edge of totally becoming something you are not.

*Imitation 10*

When we're children, our parents don't teach us to press a seashell to our ear to learn what the ocean sounds like. We're already by the sea; our feet got wet picking up the shell. We listen to a seashell to discover that the audible expulsion of something so immense, so powerful, can be re-created within a narrow, delicate canal of some other form pulled from its depths.

Still, the distinction isn't often made. Our parents don't ask us if we can hear an imitation of the ocean. They ask us, "Can you hear the ocean?" *Close your eyes. Listen.* We are amazed that, yes, here it is, clutched in our tiny hands. The complexity of life is deepened, our minds process yet another layer. And after lowering the shell away from our ear—the sound of suctioned air released—we wonder which one is truth, which one is real.

ART

On Amazon.com, there is a radio that's not really a radio available for purchase. It's a made-in-China model of a vintage wooden 1950s-looking American radio, listed under the name, "Geceyolcusu644 Europe Style Resin Radio." This "radio" contains a tiny, non-functioning "speaker" and both tuning and volume "knobs," but only exists as a reminder of the radio's original purpose: to play sound.

Collectively, as a culture, we tend to poke fun at people who unironically collect "kitschy" collectible items like these, which seem to only have a sentimental value. An imitation of a functional object—in this case, an object that transmits electromagnetic waves of radio frequency for the purposes of entertainment and communication—is inherently tacky, unless it's manufactured for children to mimic adults with.

Still, not all imitations are artless. Artists, of course, use imitation in their artwork all the time. Marcel Duchamp's famous porcelain urinal probably comes to mind. Sound artists, like Hong Kongese artist Samson Young, imitate the sounds of war though the use of drums, razors, cans of compressed air and other instruments and objects. An artist once imitated the sound of the seashore using carpet and a microphone.

So, what is the difference between a plastic "radio" and microfiber "ocean waves"?

As stated in the book *Sonic Experience: A Guide to Everyday Sounds*, edited by Jean-François Augoyard and Henry Torgue, imitation in art "implies a sense of intention on the part of the emitter." To be appropriately perceived, it also "requires the listener's knowledge of the reference." Without context, the experience might mean very little.

Duchamp also discussed how a work of art has no meaning unless a viewer brings meaning to it. (Or, in the case of sound art, a listener.) With this concept in mind, sound artists like John Cage have even used silence as art. Cage's famous 1952 composition, "4'33"" for example, consisted of a score that instructed the onstage musicians not to play their instruments throughout all three movements. Audience members sat listening to the sounds of themselves instead: suppressed coughs, cleared throats, shuffling feet.

Cage's argument was that, once "silence" is played for an audience in a concert hall or museum, the nature of nothing changes. It's something; it's an imitation of silence. Plus, who's to say that the everyday sounds of humanity aren't music?

Nevertheless, if an artist had made that cheap decorative model of a vintage radio and displayed it in the Tate Modern with a written explanation of intention, whether it would be art is debatable. Maybe this is the only thing we can understand about art and imitation: once we become aware, everything changes.

# The Sound of the Mute Button

On nights that he called us downstairs to watch a recorded clip, we settled into the faded floral-upholstered couch while our father fiddled with the VCR, fast-forwarding or rewinding a VHS tape to the exact spot. One evening, he didn't sit in his recliner like usual, instead standing an arm's length from the TV with the remote control in one hand, pointing at the screen with the other, rewinding over and over again to a scene of John Wayne swinging a chunk of plywood like a baseball bat and whacking one of a thousand bad guys across his stubbled jaw. During each replay, our father said, "Watch this, watch this, here he goes girls, bam!"

He played only the corniest clips of *The Lawrence Welk Show* for us, where white women in matching vanilla custard–colored dresses sang with frozen smiles or vaguely Italian-looking men tap danced and crooned and then he'd laugh and laugh, glancing over to gauge our reactions, hoping we were amused too. One time, he cracked up so hard at a clip of Chevy Chase losing his appetite at a bottom-dollar lunch buffet in Las Vegas that he clutched a hand to his chest and tears ran down his reddened cheeks. I locked eyes with my sister, both of us silently asking, *Should we go get Mom?*

Once each clip finished though, he lifted the remote and hit "mute."

Still, the recordings were my father's way of sharing himself with us. While we sat at the kitchen table, he watched TV. We knew not to bother him when he was stressed—he bristled at the sounds of our voices, as if they pierced his skin. But there were no formal speeches or protocol manuals. He established an unspoken set of rules for how to act—for how to be—if you wanted to maintain access to him. First rule: Everyone else is responsible for the noise and his reactions to it, so tread lightly, kids.

There were more signs that something was wrong. Sometimes, he'd switch into this deep, dominant voice and walk around our 1960s ranch home bellowing phrases such as, "Wh-yyyy, no one respects the man of the house!" or "Be-ttttt-yyy, go get me a beer!" But Betty was the name of my grandmother, and she didn't live with us. He was impersonating his deceased father's voice, and I never knew whether to laugh or hide or tell him that it was okay.

On the rare occasions that my father didn't shake his head when I asked to have friends over on a Saturday afternoon, they'd say, *Why is your dad always in the basement?* and I'd just stand there staring at my feet, unsure how to answer.

Once, I shuffled downstairs to talk to him about how I didn't want to attend the university a mile down the road—the one that he'd chosen for me—and he ignored my pleas and played a clip of Johnny Carson instead. Johnny was raising his eyebrows at the laughing audience, emphasizing the awkwardness of some moment in an interview, and he rewound the clip to the beginning at least three times. I hugged a scratchy throw pillow, took a deep breath, and tried not to cry.

The recordings on the videotapes were all mixed up. Rewind, rewind, mute, unmute. The sound garbled and the screen jumped to a clip recorded off the Iowa City local access station of a drunk guy singing "These Boots Are Made for Walkin'" at a karaoke bar. Then it'd skip again, maybe to a clip of two overweight overall-clad men in a fishing boat, one or both nicknamed Pinky, slow-talking about bait. As years went by, my sister started retreating upstairs after less than a minute and my father didn't realize how important it was that she kept leaving and he kept not asking her to stay.

I did stay and thought, *She just can't handle it,* as if this was a weakness of hers, as if my ability to shrink my decibel output to nearly nothing was a strength, or a demonstration of my ability to be good. I tolerated the constant whir of the tape rewinding and fast-forwarding because after a while my father would stop fiddling with the remote and let the tape play on low volume. The recordings of Curly getting slapped by Moe, wedding attendees slipping and falling on dance floors, men in what my father called "three-piece monkey suits" advertising used car dealerships in commercials: eventually these all revealed themselves to just be short clips taped over longer programs.

The backdrop of all his tapes were shows about nature or about the human condition: videos of loons diving into lakes, grizzlies catching salmon at the crests of waterfalls, a narrator with a soft baritone voice speaking about force and beauty while a camera panned over a bleak icy landscape at sunset. My father sipped a beer in his recliner, I covered myself with blankets on the couch, and we watched a woman in India pull strangers, one right after the other, into her bosom and bless them. Bob Ross nursed a baby bird that he kept in a box underneath his easel; scientists and art historians beamed flashlights at ancient murals in a tunnel underneath Rome. My sister was nowhere to be found and I entered a sort of TV-induced stupor, content with the quiet but wondering if I'd ever leave Iowa.

I started citing homework and friends when my father wanted me to come downstairs to watch a recording. In return, he started planning ahead of time. *It's paused right at the spot already*, he'd say, *you don't even have to wait for me to find it like last time.* My mother would sympathize when he'd emerge from the basement and shuffle around in his slippers, looking for anyone to pay attention. So, we'd stand around the TV like old times and wait for him to start the tape. Yet, now that he risked losing his audience after the clip played once, the pressure was on.

He asked us to come downstairs less and less.

My sister and I got older, moved out, and felt bitterness growing within us and pushed everyone away, including my father, including each other. I eventually stopped going home, even on holidays, so we didn't all have to acknowledge the fact that we no longer knew each other that well. I could tolerate my quiet, but not his.

My father learned how to use the computer and began emailing us links to YouTube videos instead, first to both his girls, then just to me. One email contained a video of retired couples line dancing at a bar in Oklahoma and he wrote, "I like the short guy with the potbelly, yellow shirt and hat." Another video showed a sushi chef in Japan chopping a wiggling octopus tentacle with a massive knife. The body of the email didn't have any text; he just filled in the subject line with the word "Suppah!"

Eventually he stopped sending the videos, claiming it was due to his lack of interest with the internet, and painted more instead. I stayed with my parents for two months during summer break of graduate school after a stranger I went on a date with left me broken. Even though my father and I either fought or ignored each other that summer, he gave me a plank of old barn wood and an antique window frame that he'd painted nature scenes on with a mix of oils and acrylics. He pointed out the hooks he'd screwed into the backs, saying, *See, you can hang them wherever you want in your apartment, there's a hook there, just use a nail, so you'll think of me.*

Later, he began tucking a folded-up piece of paper into my mother's birthday and holiday cards before she mailed them to us. The paper always had a weird squiggly man face drawn on it. A lopsided quotation bubble stemmed from the man's mouth that, at first, was filled with nonsensical, made-up words like, "bleeeggghhhhh," or "xxxgg-hhiii," but eventually the weird man in the drawings had quotation bubbles that read, "I love you," or "I miss you," "I wish you were here," "Come home," but we still didn't come home, we just couldn't—we couldn't even voice why—and eventually I'd open a card and there was no paper, no face, no dialogue to sound out while I stood in my socks in front of my apartment mailbox, just three letters printed after my mother's signature that read: DAD.

- - - - - - - - - - - - - - - - - - - - - - - - - - - - - - - - - - - - - - -

CHANGE

Up until around the mid-1990s, typing created a solid and mechanical "clacking" noise—almost manic-sounding in effort—followed by the loud, jingling clatter of the typewriter's carriage sliding back to align itself with the left margin of the paper. Using a typewriter was like a horse cart traveling on a brick road: it was harsh and tedious but at the same time you knew you were getting somewhere.

And then, with the introduction of computers and now smartphones, things changed.

In *The Soundscape: Our Sonic Environment and the Tuning of the World*, Canadian composer R. Murray Schafer notes that, first, the Industrial Revolution massively shifted the soundscape. Think: type-writers, sewing machines, steam engines, spinning mills, cast-iron rails, gas engines, hydraulic presses. Think: your whole existence, now disrupted and shifted by human-made noise.

Then, the Electric Revolution changed it more. The telegraph. The phone. The radio. Something mysterious referred to as "television broadcasting." As Schafer also discusses, all sounds used to emit only from their original sources. Since the invention of electroacoustic equipment though, sounds are recorded and shared around the world, even now shooting up to satellites orbiting earth and back.

As technology progresses, the list of endangered or extinct sounds grows. In 2012 three anonymous graduate students created a web-site dedicated to preserving obsolete tech-related noises, titled the Museum of Endangered Sounds. Their collection of recorded clips of soon-to-be-nonexistent noises includes:

> The jingle of a cash register
> The high-pitched and fuzzy alien tones of dial-up internet
> The "click" and "clack" of a rotary phone
> The mechanical hum of a VHS tape rewinding or fast-forwarding
> The white noise of an analog television after the antenna is unable to receive a viable transmission signal, which is caused by radio waves and electromagnetic background radiation signals, otherwise known as: STATIC

*Part
Three*

# The Sound of a Mimicker

The hurt was so bad that even the insides of my elbows ached. I was sleepless, emptied out and trapped—all of which I blamed on the city. Noise is an easier target than depression. Lying in bed next to the open window that overlooked my landlady's courtyard on the Upper East Side, I could hear:

Car horns and distant sirens
The *thrum* of air-conditioning units worked to near break-
   down by a hot summer
The high-pitched *buzz* of electricity
Rubber wheels screeching on cement

—and then—

A bird

In Manhattan, non-nocturnal birds often work the night shift due to the influence that chronic light and noise pollution have on their circadian rhythms. Nobody is sleeping well, not even the pigeons. So, when this bird broke the unwavering *hum* of my sadness two hours before Sunday's dawn, the timing didn't surprise me. The strange song did.

The bird's melody was complex and unpredictable; I'd never heard vocalizations like it before. Similar to a DJ sampling tracks, it cycled through a repertoire of beats and patterns. The bird expulsed the fast and violent percussive noise of what sounded like a jackhammer and then whistled in two simultaneous tones, high and low, high and low, its voice pure and effortless.

The next call was akin to the brash bray of a seagull. Then a *click*— clean and muted like the automatic locks on a car.

Back to jackhammer.

High and low, high and low.

A breathy whistle that sounded like wind or maybe distant traffic.

Now sliding up and down on harsh nasal notes: an ambulance siren.

Back to jackhammer followed by the *beep boop* of a cellphone.

Finally, it serenaded the neighborhood with what was unmistakably the furious cry of a car alarm.

Lying there in bed, my body was alive with the feeling of *what the fuck?* Careful not to disturb my feathered visitor, I rolled over and peeked out the window, but the neighboring brownstones' rear lights weren't bright enough to penetrate the branches of the tree where the bird was perched. Only my ears could marvel. It crooned for maybe two or three minutes more before taking off, leaving a stunned and quieter world in its wake.

The bird was, of course, a northern mockingbird. A mimicker. I confirmed this with an online search on my phone for "Mockingbirds in New York City." They're still uncommon in urban areas but have increasingly settled further north over the last century due to the spread of the invasive plants species they thrive on.

My hurt was interrupted—the sound had at least been something new and I fell into a shallow sleep. At dawn, I got up and boiled water for tea, waited for Kumar to return home from his night shift at the hospital, and wondered what to do today. The only answer: *sleep.* Still, I refused myself our bed and sat on the futon instead, where I scrolled through my earlier internet search results.

After passing dozens of YouTube videos related to mockingbirds, I found a low-quality video a woman recorded on her cellphone. In the video, a magpie—another bird capable of mimicry—enters a farmhouse through an open second-story windowsill. The woman behind the camera speaks to it in Russian. In response, the magpie vocalizes the distinct sound of a child's laugh. She coos at the bird again and it responds with the child's laugh. Coo, laugh, coo, laugh, again and again.

The laugh is high-pitched, innocent and joyful. According to the video's description, the woman raised the bird in her home in the presence of her young daughter. At some point, the bird mind-recorded this common household noise and now sang it back with remarkable perfection.

A mimicked laugh is far less jarring than the sounds of sirens or construction equipment. Still, for me, the odd bucolic scene quickly shifted into horror, and not just due to the inherent creepiness of a child's sweet giggle detached from the actual child. My depressed mind leapt to morbidity, asking, *but what if the child dies?* What if this woman's beautiful golden light of a loved girl disappears forever and all she's left with is this winged creature mocking her with the sound of her dead daughter laughing?

Imagine waking to the giggle at night—a dream turned into a nightmare.

Sitting there on the futon with phone in hand, I thought about how a bird haunting my house with ghost sounds would have me jumping from the nearest window. I was failing to thrive as is. Since moving to New York City from Boston for Kumar's residency, I'd detached from the quiet I depended on for stability. I ached to hear nature's authentic voice. I ached. And then, ringing out in the early morning hours, there it was: nature's voice in the form of the oppressive urban landscape that had me unhinged, repeated back in solo pieces.

A cruel joke.

This mimicry that had sparked me with curiosity, with life, *finally, with life*, now had me on my knees. I cried for this woman's plight with the magpie torturing her over the loss of her daughter, which I'd somehow convinced myself was inevitable. Without children of my own to imagine dying, I cried for my estranged sister and her childlike laugh; it sounds like a stream bubbling over its borders. I cried for the peace and quiet that eluded me, the sacred soundscape that my species had destroyed.

This murderous mockingbird warned me about the noises I'd endure, day after day. It sang me back the sounds of my new, bleak territory, without one imitation of hope—no wind in the forest, no lapping waves, no gentle cricket—and now look at me, brought down by a bird, my face twisted with despair, teacup shaking in my hand, spilling hot liquid onto the parquet floor.

-------------------------------------------------------------------

### DISRUPTION

Artificial light has long been the culprit for many issues: the disappearing night sky, disruption of bird migration patterns and the poor quality of our sleep. Thus, many residents of cities who've been woken by noisy avian neighbors were quick to assume that the source of birdsong at night was light pollution. Yet even though some researchers support this theory that city lights confuse birds' natural body clocks (thus causing them to be up chirping when they should be snuggled down in their nests), others believe another type of pollution might be to blame: noise.

In a 2007 study from the University of Sheffield in England, researchers measured the noise magnitude of sixty-seven locations around their city. They found that these areas were not only less noisy at night than they were during the day but were also frequently visited by a very common local bird: the robin. After studying the areas more, researchers found that the red-breasted birds singing at night were the same ones exposed to the highest levels of daytime noise pollution.

So, what was the reason for their nocturnal arias? As detailed in the study, the most probable reason is that other robins would be unable to hear them amidst the loud daytime noise. As robins sing for their survival—they call out to attract a mate and to assert their territory—the researchers argue that it's vital for them to go against their biology and stay up to communicate.

Of course, many birds have shown some impressive adaptation skills to human-made environments. In the never-ending search for crumbs, pigeons mill around in super high-decibel areas like Times Square. And in Germany researchers reported that nightingales, due to their competition with city noise, have started singing so loudly while searching for a mate that they've been recorded breaking sound regulations.

Why does all this disruption matter? Whether the reason for non-nocturnal birds suddenly working the night shift is due to light pollution or noise pollution (or conceivably both) researchers all agree on one thing: the interrupted natural rhythms results in a great deal of stress on cities' bird populations.

# The Sound of an Animal

It was difficult because I only saw him sleeping. Kumar was a deep sleeper then too; one morning after finishing a long shift, he lied down on the rug in our one-bedroom apartment and fell asleep instantly—facedown, arms flat by his sides, still in his pale blue hospital scrubs. I'd been in the bathroom washing my face and then walked back out and there he was, my possibly dead husband. I lowered myself to the floor and started shaking him because all I could think was this: *You are not leaving me here alone.*

Of course, I wouldn't have technically been alone because I had the rats. Not the mangy ones that waddled across New York City sidewalks on nights before the trash got picked up, but the domesticated ones we bought at a nearby pet store and kept in our bedroom—Ethel, Maude, and Harriet.

Our rats lived in a three-tiered cage shoved between the end of the bed and the clothes rack that we couldn't shift by even a centimeter. If the cage was pressed up against the wall, they might reach their tiny paws through the bars and grab the lamp cord, but they also couldn't be positioned too near our clothes or else they'd tear holes in my shirts. The same went for the bed—too close and they'd put their teeth to the duvet.

All three slept during the day. Snuggled together inside a woven straw tunnel, it was hard to distinguish which long, mottled pink tail belonged to which rat inside the mass of gray and white fur. Then they'd awake at sunset, exposing their amber teeth as they yawned. I liked to watch this process; it reminded me of the beauty behind being the keeper of such little souls and that those souls established a routine based on nature, even within that noisy city, within that apartment, within a cage.

After a bit of stretching and grooming, the rats stood up on their back legs and clawed at the door, demanding to be released.

I'd release them.

Originally, the rules for free time in the apartment were this: 1) No longer than twenty minutes out at a time, and 2) Constant monitoring. Yet within weeks of bringing them home, Ethel, Maude and Harriet skittered around our apartment for two or three hours with as much freedom as a cat.

They learned to climb, moving from floor to futon, futon to chair, chair to bookshelf. Harriet chased my hand if I dragged it along the top of the futon, and Ethel, so spastic, often sprinted toward me, halted, turned, snorted and jumped straight up in the air. Darting in and out, she dared me to catch her, softly nipping at my fingers if I did.

Ethel's greatest achievement was the full-body climb—a daring maneuver. She embarked on it every time that Kumar walked in the door. While he kicked off his shoes and dropped his bag and hospital ID badge on the floor, she made a great initial leap onto his shin and began the ascent with her beady eyes focused upward, nails gripping the thin material of his scrubs. She lost speed by the time she was at his stomach and struggled up his chest but triumphantly summited at his shoulder every time. Harriet, chubbier and clumsier, mimicked Ethel's actions, but only reached Kumar's thigh before dropping to the floor.

Meanwhile, Maude scurried into a hiding spot, alarmed by any new noise or movement in her environment.

I kissed Ethel and Harriet on the head every time I put them back in their cage. I cooed at them, called them "my little chicken nuggets."

But Maude backed herself into a corner whenever I got near. Sitting on the floor, I tempted her with pieces of banana or cheese, but still she retreated. If Kumar was home, he'd eventually just catch her and put her back in the cage. "Gentle, gentle, she's scared," I used to say, but he was losing his patience. The weeks kept passing and she showed little adjustment to her new life.

Unfortunately, what Maude wanted—and it's the only thing she wanted since day one—was some quiet dark place out of the way where nobody could bother her, where she couldn't be seen. If I called her name, she sought refuge underneath the broken radiator. She squealed when I held her in my lap or even just stroked her with a finger.

I didn't know how to make her better. In fact, she was only getting worse.

GETTING A PET had been my idea because I was the one crying all the time after my old dog died right before we moved to Manhattan for Kumar's medical residency. The move had been more stressful than we expected. Finding, applying for, and renting an apartment required putting down a huge chunk of my savings and him calling up friends and family to ask if they'd be guarantors, meaning, would you be potentially responsible for thousands of dollars if we were to fuck up? One evening in a hotel room in New Jersey, we joked that if our realtor asked for a kidney, we'd have to flip a coin to decide who was donating.

When we finally signed a lease for a tiny spot of New York real estate, we were too broke to go out and celebrate, but we didn't care. We watched bad TV and drank our way through a six-pack of beer instead.

At first, the decorating and acquiring of furniture—something I'd never done before in my long history of Craigslist-roommate living situations—kept me busy. Weeks later, I looked around the place, noticing how I'd organized all the books by genre, framed and hung pieces of art, assembled a table and storage units, placed plants on the windowsills, and stacked dishes in the cupboards above the World War II–era kitchenette. I was baffled by how I'd cared so much.

That summer before we got the rats, I woke up with Kumar every morning at 5:30 a.m. As he brushed his teeth and poked at the puffy skin under his eyes, I boiled water for tea, toasted bread, opened dresser drawers, opened my laptop . . .

I was trying to fool him. I was trying to fool myself.

Once he left for the hospital, I turned off the lights and crawled back into bed, seeking relief from the noise pollution of the city that

I swore was killing me. After five or six more hours, I got up. Then I cried.

Like Kumar, I also had work, but my work was just a job, just a way to get by until I could achieve something bigger, like getting a position at a magazine, or making actual progress on a book—something, anything that I could be proud of, anything that could validate my pursuit of writing. I tutored ESL students at various locations around the city, meeting them in cafés or libraries. Hired because of my bachelor's degree and fluency in English, tutoring at least forced me to leave the apartment for small bouts of time. I washed my face, wore clean clothes and my students looked pleased to see me.

My students were under the false impression that I had my shit together. They asked for my advice and always expressed curiosity about how I spent my free time—especially my Friday and Saturday nights.

"Well," I started, "first I met my husband at a bar in the East Village to have a drink. Then we met up with friends and went to a concert. Afterwards . . ."

When I reciprocated the question, they assumed my confidence and enthusiasm: "Well, first I eat the dinner . . ."

I wonder now if they knew I was fabricating a new existence just for conversation. My eyes were usually swollen, there were cuts on my forearms and the worksheets I crafted were littered with evidence, including verb conjugation sentences like these:

The woman ___ (to drink, past tense) too much alcohol
      last night.
The girl ___ (to be, present tense) lonely.
Where ___ (to be, past tense) the man go?

When I wasn't tutoring, I wandered around the city. I walked six, seven, eight miles at a time—over to the West Side, through Hell's Kitchen, down to Greenwich Village, or I voyaged straight south to the Lower East Side or even as far as Chinatown. I figured I needed to indoctrinate myself into the high-decibel culture. Or maybe I was just trying to out-pace my own decline. But eventually I quit exploring and just circled around the reservoir in Central Park. I started with a lap or two, but soon couldn't make it the three blocks from my apartment to the park entrance. Later, opening the apartment door became an insurmountable act. I paced the old, unfinished hardwood floors instead.

Sometimes, I'd find a way to smile, breathe and remind myself that everything was going to be okay, and then there I was: me. Me who wrote. Me who applied for multiple jobs each day. Me: a model of resiliency. This was just another moderate, short-lived bout of depression. I would be fine.

But soon I had to induce these moments, first with a couple of beers, then a glass or two of wine, then swigs of whiskey from the bottle we kept on the bookshelf. Later, I added weed to the routine—just a hit or two at first, then an entire bowl of weed plus swigs of Nyquil if I still felt anxious, then three cups of coffee or a small handful of caffeine pills to keep myself awake, then a combination of everything to keep me from falling off the edge.

OUR LANDLADY FIRST said "no" to a dog, then the same to a cat, and so I wasn't going to ask her about the rats. I'd decided they were our best option—fish and reptiles require expensive aquariums, hamsters seem a bit dumb, birds will wake the neighbors with their singing, but I'd read online that rats are smart, trainable, capable of emotional connection and overall great companions. We barely had room for a mini fridge, but the sacrifice of space seemed worth it.

After I sold Kumar on the idea of rats over a couple of drinks, I started mentioning the possibility to some of my students. It'll give us a chance to practice animal vocabulary, I told myself, but really, I was just excited. Most of them were shocked though, or even horrified. When they asked me, "why?" I admitted that I needed the company, because I was home alone a lot, because my husband was a first-year resident who worked eighty-hour weeks.

I didn't tell them that I had no idea what I was doing or that I was desperately lonely, partly because my husband—my only friend in this city—was too tired to even notice me anymore. I didn't tell them that I needed someone else to feed and bathe and care for because it'd become clear by three months since the move that I struggled to do these things for myself. The logic was broken, sure, but I needed something.

ONE SUMMER MORNING, Kumar and I walked into a pet store on the Upper East Side where an employee directed us to the aisle adjacent to the birds. All the rodents were housed inside small brightly lit aquariums with no toys or wheels or places to climb, and while they had dozens of dwarf hamsters and mice, there were only two rats—both listed as "rescues." They appeared to be sisters: same size, same features, similar coloring. When we asked a store clerk about them, the only thing she knew was that somebody had dropped them off.

I pressed a finger against their glass cage. "Do they bite?" I asked. The clerk shrugged. "It's possible."

Glancing at Kumar, I whispered, "Here goes nothing," and lowered a hand into the cage.

One rat, which we later named Maude, darted into a green plastic igloo, but the other, Ethel, didn't run, and instead stood up on her hind legs and nipped at my fingers. Her huge black eyes reflected the overhead lights and the outline of my face. When I pointed this out to Kumar, he said something about just being glad that her eyes weren't red, like the ones we'd seen at a pet store downtown.

When the clerk resumed stocking shelves, we mulled over the logistics of taking them home.

"Do you think they'll actually, like, help you feel better?" Kumar asked. His face looked pale. Dark circles ringed his eyes. I knew he'd rather be using this rare time away from the hospital to sleep.

I didn't have an answer, but in that moment I was out of the apartment and feeling the promise of something new—something beyond the slow, dark sadness that all my thoughts and experiences now filtered through—and so when I looked at the glass cage and the poor rat shaking inside the igloo, I wanted this decision to change things for me. For us.

I looked into his eyes and said, "Yes."

We purchased the rats, just the two at first, along with a three-tiered cage, food, a water bottle, bedding, a wheel, a straw tunnel, a hollowed-out coconut and a bunch of neon-colored wooden chew sticks. I lugged the big plastic bags of supplies home. Kumar carried the two cardboard boxes in his arms, attempting not to jostle our new pets.

It took us almost an hour to set up the cage but once we freed the rats into their new home, they sprinted up and down the wire ladders, exploring each floor and scurrying in and out of the tunnels.

We sat on the edge of the bed watching, fascinated by their spontaneity and speed. Ethel play-wrestled Maude to the ground in a fight over coconut space and I laughed. In fact, I couldn't stop laughing, which was weird, which felt a little bit like something had snapped loose, and it got to the point where tears and snot and mascara ran down my face. Kumar interpreted this as a positive response and put his arm around me, squeezed my shoulder, and said, "I think it's going to be okay." Then he fell asleep.

I QUICKLY BECAME the lady who had rats living inside her clothes.

Whenever I would let them out, Ethel would *blink blink blink* at me as if adjusting her nearly blind eyes to the world outside her cage, and then she'd leap onto my lap, always checking my pockets for crumbs.

Maude, on the other hand, didn't act out of curiosity. She acted on fear and crawled underneath my shirt into the space between my back and the futon, escaping from even the dimmest of light. Her sharp nails dug into my skin, which was now covered in swollen red scratches. But I didn't disturb her. I'd read on an online forum that this was a good method for rats to get used to the smell of their new owners. After thirty minutes or so, I'd reach around to put her back in the cage.

Initially, I expected her to squirm away from my grasp, but instead she'd clench her muscles so tightly that I'd panic for a moment, thinking she'd suffocated and died. Soon, I sat on the futon with her several times a day and told myself that she'd get used to her new living situation with more time and exposure, even though something didn't feel right. As my attachment grew, any warmth she had lessened.

Two weeks after bringing Ethel and Maude home, I visited the pet store to buy more fruit-and-nut treats and noticed a petite gray and white rat curled up alone inside the same glass cage. She was shaking. I paused to stare at her, then walked away, then walked back, then remembered what I'd read about rats being happier in a pack, just like dogs, and with one quick text message seeking approval from Kumar, I waved over a store employee. I named her Harriet and woke up to a heap of three rats inside the tunnel together the next morning. Harriet, I hoped, would somehow help Maude adjust.

AT KUMAR'S MEDICAL school graduation six months before the move, I was the fiancée mingling amongst people mostly my age or younger clothed in black robes and caps. Kumar introduced me to his peers while his family trailed behind us, also smiling and shaking hands. When he was pulled away to greet a professor, I retreated to a back wall to watch the crowd.

The women in his class, I noticed, were disturbingly good-looking, with big smiles and blown-out hair. Many of them were Indian too and I couldn't help but think about how someone else here may have been a more ideal partner for the person I loved. The men had similar charm and confidence, with shoulders back and heads high. The arena was alive with an energy that I didn't quite recognize.

I watched as all these graduates responded to inquiries about their future, the most common question being, "Where did you match?" Everyone listed programs and hospitals, possible specialties and names of new cities.

At one point, I overheard an elderly man talking to a group of three young men.

"You're all going to be so great," he said.

The choice of *be* instead of *do* seemed significant. Whether he'd chosen it purposely, I didn't know, but they replied by thanking him and nodding their heads. There was no expression of self-doubt, no reddened cheeks. They seemed to soak it all in, thinking, *yes*, we are going to be great.

I'd earned my MFA in creative writing that winter, but my peers were a more anxious group than this. Near the end of the program, we were thinking: *Teaching job at a middle school in some small town? Full-time barista? Moving back in with parents? Failed existence?* We knew that some of us would manage to accomplish what we hoped to but most of us wouldn't, because it hadn't been easy or straightforward getting to this point and our mentors made sure we understood that it wouldn't get any better.

No matching process existed; there was no predetermined next step toward success. And while I felt determined to "make it," whatever that meant, it occurred to me in that arena, for the very first time, how different my career choice was from that of the man I was following to New York.

WHEN I NOTICED that the leaves on the trees in the brownstones' courtyards below us had all changed to shades of yellow and red, it hit me that I hadn't weighed myself in several months. I got undressed and stepped onto the bathroom scale. According to the digital screen, I'd lost almost fifteen pounds. *Is that right?* I wondered, but I looked up at the mirror and there was the visible confirmation: collarbone, ribs, hipbones.

I put my clothes back on and retrieved Maude from the cage. Returning to the bathroom with rat in hand, I shut the door, turned the light off and, clutching her close, lowered myself into the empty, stained tub. The dark and quiet bathroom was the only place where Maude laid on my chest or underneath my chin. Only the noise of nearby sirens penetrated the thick walls. But after a while I could no longer be still, so I carried her back to her sisters and poured myself a drink.

KUMAR TEXTED ME every day on his walk home from work with something like, "How are you feeling today?" The question appeared innocuous at first but later I suspected that he was preparing himself for what kind of person would be greeting him at the door, or more likely what kind of person would be curled up on the futon watching TV. I stopped texting him back.

I hadn't proven myself to be a very good partner, or to use a phrase that I despise—a very good "doctor's wife." Yes, I still made money from tutoring. Yes, I cooked dinner and did all the cleaning, but mostly I took care of the rats and tried to make Maude happy. Maude with the smooth white fur. Maude with the sweet face and round tummy. Maude with all that potential if I could just get her to move forward, to acclimate, to trust.

Yet even though I had the rats to keep me company, I could barely remember any former, brighter version of myself.

My new self was interesting, at least. She smeared on lipstick and danced around the apartment alone. Or she laughed at stories she imagined telling at a party. Sometimes she told these stories out loud although it was difficult to tell what words were given air, and what words just circled her mind. Either way the rats were in on whatever she was doing, whatever *I* was doing, like they totally got my dark sense of humor—Maude especially.

On the really bad days, I liked to sit on the floor with my back against the mini-fridge and feed the rats bits of sandwiches I assembled but didn't eat. They skittered around my feet, picking up the crumbs. One week I was really into spreading peanut butter on bread. Another week I liked slicing blocks of cheese and squishing it between my fingers.

I didn't write much because I couldn't concentrate beyond a few paragraphs. Sometimes, I sat in front of a blank document for hours.

Occasionally, when I was overwhelmed with sadness, I huddled in the closet with Maude and observed that, no matter how late it was, the lights from the streets and businesses and neighbors' apartments still spilled through the windows, through the gray curtains, and worked their way into the tiny spaces between the floor and closet door and I wondered how she and I were going to escape it. If I asked this out loud, all I'd hear was Maude backing up further into the boots and umbrellas.

"I DON'T WANT to feel like a monster in my own home," Kumar said to me one night. My attempts at socializing Maude had failed. While Ethel and Harriet raced toward him every time he walked through the door, Maude let out a screech and scatter. This bothered him a lot.

"If she's not going to be social, she shouldn't be allowed out of the cage. All she does is hide," he said.

He'd been working long shifts in the Intensive Care Unit for the past two weeks and was so thin that he had to double knot the drawstring on his scrub pants.

"But if she's not allowed out of the cage," I said, "she'll never learn to be social."

I avoided his eyes; we'd had this argument before. The last time we tried to leave the apartment together, it took me nearly twenty minutes to coax her out of the closet first. Kumar probably assumed I was having trouble reaching her—in that cramped space, she had the advantage of size. But really, I was scared.

There was a new development.

Maude used to react to human touch like this: *I shall back into a corner and make myself smaller or maybe even invisible.* But that day, Maude emerged from her hiding spot and lunged toward my hand, biting down on my thumb. As she didn't break skin, that first bite seemed like a warning. The message was clear though, and only became clearer over the following weeks.

It wasn't until I offered her a corner of a milk chocolate bar that she finally succumbed and let me pluck her from the dark.

KUMAR AND I fought about Maude a lot, but one of the many other issues we fought about was my depression, which was worsened by chronic urban noise. For instance, he wanted to know why I wouldn't continue to seek help, even though I'd always had debilitating flu-like and hallucinatory reactions to the various antidepressants I was prescribed, even though the condescending demeanors of the two Upper East Side psychiatrists I saw left me feeling somehow *more* likely to contemplate the distance between the roofs and sidewalks on my walks home.

The alcohol and weed combination did help me normalize for a few hours, or as Kumar called it, "the self-medicating." (And then he'd shake the nearly empty bottle of whiskey.) But I couldn't comprehend why he cared so much anyway. After all, he was seldom at home and if he was, he was rarely awake.

I'd shout stuff like, "All you think about is work!" which was a childish accusation, really, but was also true, seeing as he wasn't mentally or emotionally capable of processing anything else beyond whatever happened in the hospital.

We were both very tired.

When Maude first started acting aggressive, I concealed it from him. I didn't tell him about the warning bites or about the real bites that followed, where her incisors sliced through my skin and drew blood. I internalized all these tiny assaults—all these transfers of weak, negative energy. Maude, now territorial, attacked me simply because I reached my hand into the cage to change their water or to let Ethel and Harriet crawl up my arms. Kumar asked about the bandages on my hands but I made up excuses. When Maude started biting *him*, I could no longer be the keeper of this strange secret.

Sweet little Maude was growing bolder and more hostile every day and—more dangerously—she was inserting herself into our marriage. Kumar called the biting "vicious." I said she was "projecting." Both of us realized that having a rat sink its teeth into your flesh daily was no way to live. But we also couldn't agree on a solution. "Should we just get rid of her?" I yelled at him. "Find her a new home? Euthanize her? Set her free to die in Central Park?"

When I listed these suggestions with my arms up and eyebrows raised, Kumar sighed and shook his head. To find her a new owner and separate her from her family—her pack of fellow rats, the two other little souls that she clung to night and day—seemed almost more awful than discreetly releasing her underneath a bush near the Sheep Meadow.

Furthermore, who in New York City was looking for a highly unstable rat?

BY LATE FALL, Maude was only allowed out for free time in the empty, ancient bathtub, but I ached with guilt. She slid around the tub, confused, squeaking, her paws unable to get a firm grip against the cast iron. Yet, if I put a towel down for her, she would swiftly push it up against the side to use it to climb out.

Maude used to do better in the presence of Ethel and Harriet; she intermittently trailed them around the apartment, her nose nearly touching the tip of their tails, not wanting to fall behind. I believed that Maude wanted to be good. To be happy. To be in on the game, the chase, the wrestling match. But she had no idea how to achieve those things here, in this place. Or maybe she was just broken, like me.

Once, after thirty minutes of sitting cross-legged on the bathroom floor to monitor her, I got up and pulled on the oven mitts—the most effective tool I'd come across for handling an aggressive rodent. At first, she crouched near the drain, waiting to be picked up, possibly? But no—in a flash, she rushed me, nipping my forearm just above the mitt. The pain came harsh and fast, and my blood stained her white fur. In that moment, I wanted to throw her out our second story window and get back into bed and cry. Instead, I managed to grab her with both mitts, turned her over on her back and attempted for the twentieth time or so to make her submit. I waited for minutes on end; I took slow, calm breaths. All she did was fight. So, I carried her back to the cage as she screamed and squirmed, biting at the thick fabric protecting my hands.

I had totally failed her somehow.

Kumar returned home while I was cleaning the wound on my

forearm. He paused in the bathroom doorway, staring. His jaw was clenched; his black hair now peppered with white although he wasn't even thirty yet.

"What are we doing here?" he asked. He rubbed his temples and then pressed his hands over his eyes. I wasn't sure if he was expecting an answer.

Eight hours later, he went back to work with a look of desperation, almost as if he hoped when he returned home the next morning, we wouldn't be there anymore—as if he hoped Maude and I would just disappear.

IT WAS ON a Thursday evening when Kumar dragged himself through the door looking like a man I didn't know anymore. We didn't talk, but he set his bag down and pulled me in for a hug. It was a long hug, a reminder that neither one of us had given up yet. Then he collapsed onto the futon.

I took off his shoes.

I covered him with a blanket.

I swallowed the disappointment stuck in my throat, born from the realization that another day would go by without us spending more than a minute together.

I took a shot of whiskey.

Ethel and Harriet tugged at the socks on my feet. They'd already ripped holes in them because when they didn't get any attention from Kumar, they sought it from me. I needed to get to Midtown for a late tutoring session, so I picked them both up—one in each hand— calling them "my little chicken nuggets" before carrying them to the cage.

When I entered the bedroom, my stomach dropped. The cage door was open and Maude was gone. I somehow failed to latch it properly.

Tiptoeing back into the main room, I found her holed up behind the radiator. She tensed upon my approach but remained still. Grabbing a jar of peanut butter, I dipped a finger in and placed a blob about a foot away from her.

"Come out and get it, little *schweetiee*," I whispered.

She wasn't interested.

I thought about just leaving her there since I needed to meet my student. "Smoke her out" was a term we'd used before—eventually she'd need water and food and the company of her sisters. But I'd have to wake Kumar and tell him to watch out for her since she was liable to dart out and bite his feet if he got up to use the bathroom.

And telling him that Maude was on the loose would start yet another fight.

Ten minutes later, I was on my hands and knees trying to coax Maude out and the frustration was building. My student would be waiting for me, I'd have to race out of the subway and down the street and arrive sweaty and out of breath, because somehow this job still mattered to me, because I had to do *something* with my life, achieve *something* in this city.

I stood up and told myself not to cry. Examining the space between the wall and radiator, I realized that I might be able to reach down and pull her out, but it was tight. There was no room for my hand if I wore the oven mitt.

Not wanting to surprise her, I *clicked* my tongue, said her name and tapped my fingers against the plaster. Maude glanced up at me but didn't bolt. I hoped it was a sign of surrender.

I lowered my hand into the crevasse, wondering if it'd be more difficult to remove my arm than it was to get in. My fingers touched her back and I stroked her fur before carefully wrapping my hand around her torso. She wiggled out of my grasp but didn't bite. I touched her again, this time attempting to lift her out on my open palm, like a rat on an elevator.

At the moment I slipped my fingers underneath her belly, she bit down on my index finger. Hard.

What exited my mouth was the sound of an animal. It was a noise I'd never made before, an ancient and organic squealing scream of fear, and I instinctively tugged my arm back, scraping the entire length of my forearm against the rusty metal.

I started to swoon before I even saw the blood. My throat was tight with nausea; my skin was pulsing both hot and cold. Suddenly, Kumar was at my side. I could hear him swearing.

I clutched my injured hand in the other as if it was a poor stunned bird I'd found on the sidewalk and stumbled toward the bathroom. Splotches of blood on the parquet marked my path. As I leaned over the cool white sink, the cast iron stained red. My hand tingled. She'd bit deep, bone deep, and the whole finger swelled.

Kumar was still swearing, except now he was twisting on the cold tap water and forcing my finger underneath it.

"I can't do this anymore," he said. I looked up into the medicine cabinet mirror and was met with the reflection of my own pale and sweaty face.

"Okay," I said.

"Okay she's done?" he asked without pause.

I swallowed but my throat was too tight to respond, so I sentenced her to death with a nod.

KUMAR KILLED MAUDE in the bathroom as swiftly and humanely as he could. He'd worked with rodents in research labs in the past; it was one quick *pop* and over. I was so weak, so cowardly, in those final moments that I didn't even tell her goodbye. I didn't press her against my chest and whisper that I'm sorry. Instead, I got as far away as I could in that little apartment, humming a song to distract myself, pushing all my weight against the old, heavy bedroom door as if it might burst open and expose me to all that pain. That noise. To everything I was still trying to hide from. Ethel and Harriet sprinted around the cage, up and down the wire ladders, searching for their sister with an intensity I'd never witnessed before.

Rats are very intelligent creatures.

I'd read that rats should always view the dead body of another member of the pack so they understand that they aren't coming back. I didn't want Ethel and Harriet waiting for her to return or to think that Maude just disappeared and that they too could be disappeared at any moment. But by the time I remembered this advice and left the room, Kumar was already out the door and headed down the stairs, carrying a trash bag. I didn't slip on my shoes; I didn't follow him.

The next night, after Kumar left for work, I got stuck on this idea of "a viewing" and debated whether to go out to the garbage cans, locate the bag that contained Maude's body, and bring her back upstairs. I'd open the bag, set it on the floor and let the rats discover her on their own, saying, "See? She just died like that. Right there. We don't know why."

The garbage wouldn't be picked up until the following morning. I wondered how decayed her body would be.

I mulled this over while I made a sandwich and then kneaded it between my hands, squeezing it through my fingers like it was play-dough or mud. Ethel and Harriet skittered around, gobbling up the remains off the floor.

When all the food was eaten, the rats climbed up my bare legs and scratched my skin as they slid back down. Climb and slide. Repeat. Repeat. I could hear ambulances racing through the busy streets. Car horns honked. Some restaurant a couple blocks away was blasting music. I didn't know what I was doing here.

*If I could somehow just resurrect her . . .* I thought and took a hit of weed to stop myself from crying.

A few hours later, I crawled into the closet—the quietest space in the apartment—and didn't wriggle back out until the next morning when the sunlight lit up its dark corners. I told myself that I had to begin again, that I had to try to change. I could hear Kumar's slow, heavy footsteps on the apartment building's stairs, *up up up*, coming toward the door. Rising to my feet, I turned on the stove to boil water for tea and ran my fingers through my hair.

"You're up," he said, his voice lighter than usual.

"I'm up," I said.

We embraced, he whispered a joke and I smiled, even forced myself to laugh, but from the bedroom I could hear the rats scampering around their cage, squeaking and snorting, begging to be let out.

Here are twenty facts about the noise in New York City:

1. As documented by the *PEW* Research Center in 2018, noise levels can easily reach 95 decibels in midtown Manhattan.
2. For context, the U.S. federal government recommends that public spaces maintain an average of no more than 70 decibels.
3. For further context, the European Union recommends an average of no more than 50 decibels.
4. The noise level behind a garbage truck is 100 decibels.
5. New York City's nonemergency call service line, 311, receives fifty thousand calls a day. The number one complaint from callers is noise.
6. Sometimes it's so loud that people report turning up their personal acoustic output in response—their music, their television, the volume of their own voice.
7. This is understandable given that, while using the social app Soundprint, users in New York City have recorded noise levels as high as 90 decibels in restaurants and bars.
8. (A.k.a. we're all competing to be heard.)
9. As reported by CityLab in 2019, the corner of Canal and Hudson Street may be the loudest place in New York City, particularly during rush hour. An estimated 1,260,000 vehicles a month use it.
10. The noise doesn't just stem from rubber tires on cement; there's also the honking, the exhaust pipes, the construction noise, the brakes, the downshifting trucks, the music . . .
11. According to the Centers of Disease Control and Prevention, any noise over 80 decibels—depending on the amount of exposure—can cause irreversible hearing loss.
12. The city's many anti-noise advocates push for the revision of noise codes, greater community oversight and more studies on the effects of noise.

13. They also file lawsuits against construction and helicopter companies, as well as other notorious noise polluters, but the lawsuits often drag on for years.

14. In the meantime, the sound of an approaching subway car has been recorded as over 100 decibels.

15. Some of these anti-noise advocates have described noise pollution as "the new second-hand smoke." In 2019 the *New Yorker* even proposed that noise pollution is the next major public health crisis.

16. Yet, in New York City's new Green Deal, which calls for the state to eliminate greenhouse gases by 2050, there is no mention of noise pollution.

17. When you pass by a jackhammer, you're exposed to 130 decibels.

18. Some New Yorkers share their favorite "secret" quiet spaces in the city on online social sites.

19. Sirens from a police car or ambulance? 120 decibels.

20. Simultaneously, they also lament that residents and tourists alike eventually overrun those sacred spaces, thus raising the din.

# The Sound of a Whisper

Two years after moving to New York City, I logged onto the site Meetup.com and created a local group for people who have Autonomous Sensory Meridian Response, or ASMR. As far as I knew, I'd never met someone else with ASMR before. I wanted to discuss the experience in person and maybe further understand why I had this response; I wanted to see if I shared any traits with others who had it. But as I crafted a group description about "tingles" and "physical reactions to sound," doubt seeped in. This condition—if you can call it that—felt secretive, like I'd be revealing too much of myself by posting this shit online.

Even as a child I knew there was something inherently embarrassing about my ASMR. It's a private experience. A body experience. And it occurs under the most intimate of circumstances: one person does something minute and mundane, like brush their hair or shade in a figure drawn with crayons, and my body reacts to it as if I'm undergoing hypnosis. I simply . . . sink.

Of course, a similar response occurs during the crescendo of a powerful piece of music. The hair on my arms rises, my scalp tingles and my eyes well with tears while my throat tightens. Music is created for an audience though, often with the purpose of beauty. Thus, most people can relate to my physical response to music, referred to as auditory-tactile synesthesia. Yet, I'd never met anyone who experienced the same euphoria from, say, listening to someone stacking and sorting plastic buttons, or flipping through the paper in a three-ring binder.

This was my hope then. Through this group, I'd be able to engage in conversations about how my body reacted to everyday sounds without having to find the words to explain, to create comparisons, to find some understanding in another person's face.

Meaning, I wanted to find my people—my fellow sound-sensitive weirdoes.

After finishing the group description and paying the small set-up fee, I thought, this is New York City, the likeliest place in the world to find other people who experience the same thing that I do. I envisioned a group of calm, quiet, likeminded individuals, sitting around a table in a café, sipping tea and discussing how we enjoyed birdsong as much as the sound of long manicured fingernails tapping against a smartphone screen. We'd share stories about our first memories of ASMR and when we discovered that we're not the only ones. I imagined us laughing at mutual experiences, our cheeks reddening a little while discussing "tingly sensations."

But the gathering would be open and relaxed and therapeutic; we'd share what sounds we'd fallen in love with over the years, sounds that made us feel safe and whole, like:

1. The sound of creasing a piece of paper with a thumbnail
2. Open palms pressing against a plush folded towel
3. That vibrating ring made by setting the dog's ceramic water bowl onto a tile floor
4. Stirring a pot of extra-creamy fettucine alfredo
5. That sudden release of air after peeling back the foil top of a new can of ground coffee

This group, I suspected, might also attract other transplanted New Yorkers who physically ached and vibrated from all the noise pollution, who pulled on headphones and listened to YouTube videos created for the explicit purpose of triggering ASMR to unwind. This experience, I thought, could be more than just a fluke. Perhaps it's an inherited trait that helps people like me escape.

I FIRST STUMBLED upon the term "ASMR" in 2012 while in my early twenties and attending graduate school in Boston. Previously, the "tingles" only happened at random.

During the second semester of my MFA, my department hired me for an administrative position. The job was menial; I sat behind a desk and gave students directions to professors' offices or passed along messages. Occasionally, I was asked to input data on a spreadsheet or sort through piles of old literary journals. Otherwise, I read.

One afternoon, an undergraduate stopped at the desk and asked if their professor was holding office hours. He wasn't. After handing them a sticky note and pen, my mind perked at the sound of the pen scratching against the paper, coupled with the movements of their hand. My face and scalp tingled, as if an invisible feather was tickling me. Just this simple act—pen, paper, writing—transported me into a super relaxed state. I was sleepy and smiley, yes, but also a better version of myself. A happier version. From my station behind the desk, I fought back against the heaviness of my eyelids.

The experience didn't last for more than a minute, but during that time I released all the anxiety and tension I'd been carrying. After the student left, I felt like I'd just awakened from an hour-long nap.

That evening, as I walked toward the Boylston Street T station, an epiphany hit: maybe other people experience this thing. Maybe other people also connect to sound in a deeper, stranger way, or list the sounds they love in their journal like I do.

After getting back to my apartment, I opened my laptop and googled "tingly sensations" and "writing." The search engine came up with thousands of hits, mostly related to sex. It took twenty minutes or so of playing around with keywords and scrolling through sites, but I was determined to find out if anyone else had ever reported similar feelings online.

And that's when I discovered my first ASMR video.

In the YouTube video, a woman from Majorca shows her nail polish collection to the camera while whispering about the different colors. Listening through headphones, I watched as she plucked a small glass bottle from a plastic makeup bag, untwisted the lid (the dried nail polish around the rim crackling as it broke) and held the thin brush near the camera lens. "This is a sparkly pink," she whispered before plunging the brush back into the paint. Next, she reaches her hand inside the bag (the glass bottles all clinking together) to reveal another hue.

Tingles seeped out of my scalp, surrounded my head in an aura of pleasure and trickled down my spine into the nerves in my arms and legs. The sensation was reminiscent of the feeling of being massaged: that release of tension and pain that occurs after someone skillfully rubs your shoulders, your back, your feet—some area that, once relaxed, makes you feel like a new person; a person who was, until that moment, so caught up in their meaningless, hard, stressful little earthly existence that, once this release happens, you're suddenly aware of feelings, sounds, beauty, your simultaneously tiny and massive place in the universe, and viewing it all while in a pleasantly groggy, floating state—a state in which you are safe, even childlike.

*Childlike*: The video also immediately reminded me of how, whenever my sister and I visited one of our favorite cousins, she would rummage through her makeup collection to show us her new purchases. Removing her lipsticks from their pristine boxes, she'd create a line of swatches on the back of her hand—the burgundy, rose and auburn pigment melting into her skin. Or she gently popped open the plastic lids of blush and eye shadow palettes, tapping a fingernail against each pot of color and explaining their tones and qualities in a hushed voice. The crescendo occurred when she lifted her makeup brushes from their spot on her vanity. She grazed the brushes—all as soft as rabbit fur—against our cheeks or hands, which sounded like a gloved hand sweeping away fresh powdery snow.

Now, I could access this experience on the internet. By being able to tap into these feelings with a *click* of a button, I had harnessed a sensation that I thought was only available spontaneously.

The number of ASMR videos I found on YouTube was astonishing too, even though I later learned that the term had only been coined around 2010. There were triggers for drawing sounds, paper sounds, whispering, painting nails, painting pictures . . . triggers for bedtime story reading, writing on a chalkboard and a dry erase board, folding towels, folding cloth napkins, tapping fingernails. As soon as a video ended, I'd restart it or just click on another suggested video that popped up. I was on a seemingly endless loop of what I knew, to the outside world, looked like crazy. But the more I watched, the more my mind quieted.

Looking back at this scenario, I'm envious of this past version of myself—the ASMR video virgin. I'll likely never experience such powerful tingles again. Not only could I submerge into these sublime feelings of relaxation whenever I wanted or needed to, but I now had an explanation for my experiences—or at least a community of people out there in the vast reaches of the internet that reported the same reactions as me. I wasn't alone. I was part of something. Kind of.

6. The crunch created by ambling across snow covered with a thin frozen crust
7. Steady rain hitting a single-paned glass window
8. Cracking the crystallized sugar atop a ramekin of crème brûlée with a spoon
9. The burst of those air-filled pouches of bubble wrap
10. Rattling a pocketful of smooth round stones

At first, only two people joined my New York City ASMR group. This was a relief; I had an excuse to give into my anxiety and not set up an in-person group meeting. But after another month, a dozen more people joined. I procrastinated through January but eventually forced myself to schedule the first meeting.

The February weather was forecasted for snow, sleet and wind, but it didn't matter. Even if no one showed up and I spent an hour alone at a table with a handwritten sign that read "ASMR Group," I had put this event in motion and was seeing it through. A small accomplishment, sure, but that winter had me on my knees. I spent too much time alone in the apartment, too much time crying, and I was unable to overcome or even acknowledge my depression. I needed quiet. In daydreams, I created a "restart" button; it woke me up all fresh and new in a field of snow, the land so hushed that you could hear the trees creaking in the wind.

Only three people RSVP'd.

Still, on the scheduled Sunday afternoon, I walked to our meeting place: a café located in a less busy, unhip area of the city. Given that we would be chatting about something we all used to experience privately, it seemed appropriate to choose a spot where there was less chance for others to be listening in. I also timed my arrival to be only a few minutes early. I didn't want to sit there waiting, my palms growing sweatier each time the bell on the door jingled.

Upon entering the café, I noticed its empty chairs. Only three or four patrons had trudged through the slush to buy a mediocre coffee and stale bagel, including a man I recognized from his Meetup.com profile picture. He'd listed his name as Fred and appeared to be in his seventies. Fred wore the same clothing he'd donned in the picture: red messenger cap, plaid scarf, dark blue peacoat. His gray hair stuck out from underneath his cap in thick, greasy chunks. I thought, *there is still time, you can just turn around and leave and no one will ever know.* But Fred was harassing a young woman studying at a corner table who looked somewhat like me in the way that she was also white, and her hair was also a shade of brown.

"You're telling me you're not her?!" Fred yelled.

She shook her head and frowned.

I walked over and tapped Fred on the arm, saying "hello," but he didn't notice and continued yelling at the woman. She pointed at me, urging him to look over his shoulder. When he did, I caught a whiff of his breath and instinctively backed up.

"Oh, there you are," he said, grinning.

At the counter, Fred couldn't find any cash in his wallet to pay for his latte, so I reluctantly turned over a $10 bill to the barista and paid his tab. Still hoping that the two other confirmed guests might show up, I gestured at a cluster of tables that had several open seats. Another woman seated near the window shot me an empathetic look, silently asking, *do you need help?* I responded with a thin but reassuring smile.

From an outsider's perspective, I imagined this situation looked like a blind date from hell. It certainly felt like one.

While removing my hat and scarf, I took a deep breath and asked Fred about this topic I'd never discussed with another sound-sensitive person before.

He gave the answer I feared was coming: He'd never heard of ASMR before.

"Oh," I said. "You do realize this is a meet-up about ASMR?"

He responded by taking a long sip of the drink I bought him and clearing his throat. Then, he began explaining to me how marijuana is legal in Amsterdam.

"Yes, I've been there," I interrupted, trying to change the conversation.

"But were you there in the sixties?" Fred responded. He didn't follow up with any details, instead just shaking his head and repeating the phrase "crazy times."

As Fred then began reminiscing about his move from Europe to Albuquerque forty years earlier, I thought, perhaps this is a sign. Perhaps there is a god and they're telling me that, whatever I'm looking for, I'm not going to find it here. Underneath the table, Fred's knees brushed against mine and I pulled my chair back, inching further away from him. He only leaned in closer and rubbed his boot against my shoe. My Iowan politeness had been taken advantage of long enough. As Fred started talking about best strategies for stealing shopping carts through a mouthful of blueberry muffin he'd pulled out of his pocket, I decided I didn't have to put up with him, whether he was elderly and lonely or not.

After setting down my half-finished coffee and pulling on my mittens though, a young man in his mid-twenties walked in, blinking at me. I recognized him from his photo too: he'd RSVP'd.

"Is this the ASMR group?" he asked. His eyes darted nervously around the room.

I sighed, smiled and told him it was. As I tugged my mittens back off, the young man removed his winter coat to reveal a dress shirt drenched in perspiration. Beads of sweat dripped down his temples and cheeks, pausing at the end of his chin until he wiped them away with his sleeve. His hands trembled and his face turned a dark shade of red as he said, "So, yeah, I like ASMR."

"You seem to be perspiring an awful lot, huh?" Fred said.

I thought, this poor, young, moist man suffering a probable panic attack is the first person I've ever met in real life who, to my knowledge, also experiences what I experience.

I tried to open a dialogue. I asked how he'd discovered that ASMR is a "thing." What's the feeling like for him, how often does he watch ASMR videos, does he have any favorite YouTube channels, what are his favorite sounds? He responded with muffled one-word answers and dabbed his forehead with napkins procured from the café counter. Fred seemed jealous at my change in attention and tried to veer the conversation back to shopping carts, but I ignored him.

Finally, the young man lowered the napkin pressed to his face and said in a slow, deliberate voice: "For me, ASMR is like porn. I like watching women paint their toenails and touch their hair."

Even Fred went silent. I nodded, said something like, "well okay then," stood up, grabbed my stuff and waved "goodbye" as I marched out the door. I hadn't even gotten my arms through my coat sleeves, but the frigid air meant freedom and I took a deep inhale. A moment later though, I jumped as a man grabbed my arm—it was Fred, smiling coyly, his yellow teeth even more apparent in the dim sunlight.

"You're ending this thing already?" he asked.

I yanked myself free of him and jogged across the street, pretending not to hear as he yelled after me, asking if he could come back to my place for "a nightcap." It wasn't even 3:00 p.m.

IF THAT MEETING hadn't gone so, so stupidly bad, here are more favorite sounds that I maybe would have shared:

11. Pouring a can of seltzer into a glass of ice
12. Walking across fallen autumn leaves on a sharp day

13. Water bubbling inside an electric teapot
14. Typing on a laptop with keys that emit a crisp but muted click
15. A loved person, a woman, a sister, *whispering*, pushing air out their throat but not connecting it with sound, thus only making the molecules vibrate, a.k.a. the highest form of trust

Shortly after the failed meeting, something tragic happened: my ASMR faded. I put on my headphones and played my favorite YouTube videos, but the tingles didn't come. The trancelike state was absent too. I just felt bored, or even aggravated, while listening to the sounds of someone sketching or painting or whisper-reading a book to the camera.

I'd immersed myself in ASMR videos for over two years and now the effects had drastically lessened. My reactions to sound used to be a mystery. *A student writing a note to their professor, that scratchy sound of the pen against the paper* . . . Now, I'd killed my body's own magical coping mechanism. I should have seen it coming though. Like any drug, you must consume more and more over time to achieve the same response. I'd done it before with other substances—beer, whiskey, weed, sleeping pills. Now, binging on these videos left me feeling nothing but disgusted with myself.

Go outside, I thought. Go do something with your life.

Still, I was deeply frustrated and distraught, especially since this wasn't the first time sound had betrayed me, and not just in the form of chronic human-made noise. When I was younger, I went through periods of time when certain sounds made me squirm, like the sound of chewing. For years, I didn't mind the sound, but around the time I was twelve years old, listening to others eat was my own nails on a chalkboard nightmare.

To bite, to break down, to swallow food: that all creates its own unique song of destruction and consumption—an act that is, by nature, loud. Yet, it was almost the suppression of the sound of chewing that triggered me more than unbridled chewing, smacking and swallowing. When biological need meets the rules of etiquette in the form of eating, the *loud* becomes *muted*. To me, it sounded like people trying to distance themselves from the reality of being in a body.

For that short time that I experienced a hatred of certain sounds—or misophonia—the noise made by my mother chewing, especially, was so offensive that I took it personally. It was a selfish, immature reaction. But as a kid suffering through the early stages of puberty, it was as if my mother's chewing represented the parts of her personality that I couldn't stand: small bites, close-mouthed, very polite. It all felt so stifled, controlled, repressed, buttoned-up. To sit there without screaming or at least covering my ears took all the limited self-control I'd developed by that age.

Now, as an adult, I didn't exactly hate the ASMR videos that I'd listened to hundreds of times before. But it was like my body now threw a temper tantrum in response to the sounds. I squirmed. I hummed. I ripped my headphones off.

The only video that retained enough magic to soothe me was another upload from the woman from Majorca. I didn't feel any tingles, but the sounds still created a feeling of peace. In the video, she reads aloud from a book about Japanese geishas. Like all her videos, the production is amateur: the camera is overly zoomed in, we only see partial images of the book, the recording cuts off and starts again. But she taps her long, decorated nails against the hard cover of the coffee table book—creating a quick *thud*—or squeaks her fingertips against its big glossy paper. She also turns each page slowly, making sure she milks it for the sound, before grabbing a handful of pages and flicking them against her thumb, like she's shuffling cards. She smacks her lips a little and reads a couple sentences here and there.

Her voice is so kind and honest that I trusted her. She was my friend. My sister. She ran a finger underneath a photo caption and then, in a simultaneously wet and breathy whisper, began to read. Even though I watched that video at least a hundred times, those thirty seconds still felt like a secret. She was reading me this book at night, both of us tucked into bed, and we should have been asleep hours ago, but if we're quiet enough, this moment won't ever end.

16. The *pop* of a new waxy lipstick as it's released from its metallic tube
17. The eerie call of a wood thrush breaking dusk's stillness with a long two-toned note
18. Steam hissing from a hot iron
19. Echoes of a loon call across a lake in Minnesota
20. Dripping water—that rounded *brop, brop, brop*—reverberating through the walls of a cement tunnel

I still haven't shared my first memory of ASMR with another person. That's because, after the failed initial meeting with the shitty men and the concerned looks from strangers, I decided not to try again. Instead, I let the account grow defunct, even as the group gained more members, even as those members wrote me messages, asking when the next meeting would be. I'd bled my therapeutic responses to sound dry and, more importantly, I decided I didn't need it anymore. Not like I used to. I was figuring out other ways to relieve my depression— namely, with the help of meditation, exercise and a therapist.

There remains something unique about my body's innate ability to relax its sad, anxious, over-stimulated mind though, even if the experience has diminished as I've grown older. Listen, I don't remember if someone ever hurt me or, if so, *who* hurt me, hurt her, hurt us, but I can describe the first time I entered a state of sound-responsive hypnosis as if I'm reading it off a piece of paper. It's all there.

I was young, maybe four years old. I was with my mother and sister in a department store. My mother was doing some last-minute holiday shopping. Christmas music played over the speakers. Fake pine trees decorated with tinsel lined the walls. And behind the gift-wrapping department counter, a man in an elf costume removed my mother's purchases from the plastic bag. For a man dressed so silly, he took his job very seriously. Every action was deliberate and precise: measuring the paper along the side of a ruler, slicing it with a pair of heavy metallic scissors, folding the crinkly colorful wrapping, ripping and applying clear tape.

(He used, I realized, the same amount of delicateness with our packages that I'd seen our Methodist pastor use when handling a gold communion cup. His manner suggested that the box contained something expensive and fragile, perhaps an item that should be cherished, although the box most likely contained a few pairs of socks.)

I couldn't get enough of it—the crunchy sounds of the paper being manipulated coupled with the flowery movements of his hands. Red plastic ribbon swishing as it was unraveled from its long spool. The top of my head began to feel prickly, like someone was lightly tapping their fingertips against my scalp. By the time he began curling the ends of the ribbon on each present with a quick swipe of the open blade of his scissors, waves of pleasurable sensations were washing up and down my spine.

The spell was broken as soon as we left, but I still felt groggy on the walk to the parking lot. Before I had words for it, I thought of this sensation as The Escape.

Maybe my ASMR will come back. Maybe I'll hear the scratch of a pencil or the high-pitched *clink* of glass and get the tingles. But I don't think it will. I figured out how to live without it. Maybe others have as well. I don't know. Quiet sounds still soothe me. Some noises still make me cringe or even turn my skin slick with cold sweat. And when I need it most, strangers on YouTube whispering into microphones remind me to breathe.

21. Soft gusts of air stirring spring's new leaves and grasses
22. Ocean waves pulsing against layers of sediment and rock
23. My sister's high-pitched laugh
24. The white noise of static emitted by the analog TV after the station signed off at midnight
25. Pages of a book rustling as they turn, followed by the windy thump of a hardcover book closing

## ASMR

Autonomous Sensory Meridian Response (ASMR) is a little studied sensory phenomenon that causes pleasurable, relaxing, tingling sensations in the head or scalp that can also extend down the body through the spine and into the limbs. This phenomenon occurs in response to certain triggers, including painting, drawing, whispering, soft speaking, brushing, scratching, tapping, folding, page turning and many others. While watching ASMR videos, people also experience a calming, soothing effect. Many even report a lessening in their symptoms of depression, anxiety, insomnia and PTSD.

In 2018, in the first study of its kind, researchers from the University of Sheffield examined the physiological changes that occur in people when they experience this phenomenon. Half of the study's participants claimed to experience the "tingles;" the other half did not. Participants' heart rates were monitored as they watched both ASMR and non-ASMR videos. They found that, when watching ASMR videos, those with ASMR experienced greater reductions in their heart rates than those who did not. During interviews and surveys after watching the videos, those with ASMR also reported a significant increase in positive emotions, including relaxation and "feelings of social connection."

In their conclusive remarks, the researchers compared their findings to the effects of music therapy and mindfulness exercises. In all these cases, sound is the trigger for a healthy physiological response.

There's more: A 2015 questionnaire-based study of 475 people who experience ASMR found that 5.9 percent of participants also experience synesthesia—a neurological condition in which the brain processes data with two or more senses at once. This led the researchers to question whether the "tingles" could potentially be considered a form of "sound-emotion synesthesia." Either way, based on the shared testimonies from these studies, as well as the millions of ASMR videos on YouTube, it seems likely that ASMR is an ingrained, natural trait.

But perhaps there's also something cultural here. In a time when community and intimacy are being replaced by screens, the massive international popularity of ASMR videos could be a reaction to loneliness. Modern life can be so frantic and isolating that we've forgotten the beauty in hushed, gentle and empathetic connections. Apparently though, as the preliminary research done on ASMR demonstrates, our bodies remembered.

# The Sound of a Split Throat

If you were raised in the United States, adults maybe taught you that birds *chirp*, *cheep*, or *tweet*. In South Korea, children are taught to mimic birdsong by saying, *jjek jjek*. Children in Germany say, *tschilpen* or *zirpen*. In Japan, they're taught *chun chun*. In the Spanish language, it's *pío*, like *peee-oh!* In Turkish, it's *jick jick*. Italian: *chip*. Swedish (my favorite): *pip pip*.

The sound of a bird letting off a simple one or two-syllable call is likely closer to a combination of these imitations, depending, of course, on the bird. But for some more complicated songs, there's a component that no human can mimic. This is because birds vocalize using an organ called a syrinx, which is located where their tracheas split into two bronchial tubes. Due to this anatomical difference, birds often produce disparate pitches at once.

Some birds, like a wood thrush, can even sing both a rising and falling note simultaneously, which looks something like this:

```
                    ti
              ti
         ti
    ti
    re
       re
          re
             re
```

But here is the truth: Birds do not sing just because they're happy or to find a mate. They primarily vocalize to communicate or declare their territory, meaning one of the principle aural examples of the word "serene" (along with babbling brooks, ocean waves and soft breezes) may merely be the avian equivalent of dogs barking from behind their fences, signaling to the world that this plot of land has been locked down, *bitch*.

If I were a bird, if I could sing through a syrinx, I'd simultaneously declare my love for you and warn the world against touching you. You with your black hair struck with silver, your thick-chested and narrow-hipped body, the politeness that creates a distance between you and The Others. You. My husband. Mine. Yours was a childhood of taunts and threats via white kids and now you smile, knowing that the world will mark you down as benevolent, as *so friendly—a doctor, nonetheless!*—without ever knowing that you could strike faster than a baby can mimic a *chirp*.

In one pitch, I'll sing your power: a warning by description alone. I'll tell the tale of how I once asked you to perch on top of me and wrap your hands around my neck, just so I could see what that path out of this world is like. My blood beat heavy in my ears, sensing death. In the other pitch, I'll sing your strength: *but he couldn't squeeze.* They'll know by my tone that this compassion isn't granted to those who dare flit over our boundaries. Us first. Flock second.

How much do you remember of that one spring evening, a year after we got married at the courthouse in Lower Manhattan, when you drank too much Chianti at my friend's intimate and formal wedding rehearsal dinner in Westchester? I side-glanced you throwing back the dark red liquid like it was post-run Gatorade and I thought, *well this will be very interesting.*

Touching your arm, you may recall how I said "slow down there, big fella" in front of my friend's other friends. I was trying to keep it light, keep it no big deal, but you were hell-bent on public self-destruction. One side of my friend's family is Taiwanese, the other side Dutch, her husband is Jewish, and you were there, the Indian guy no one knew, an extension of me, making a wedding toast without point, coherence or end. Seated in my chair, I never once loosened my grasp on your elbow. It was as much a plea as it was a mother's hand steadying you before the inevitable fall.

You were blackout drunk, so I'll remind you what happened next: after stumbling out of the restaurant, you cycled between laughter and tears. I managed to retie your shoes and straighten your tie but, on the ride back to Harlem, you cleared the train car by vomiting rehearsal dinner and two bottles of wine all down your shirt and pants. I wiped your mouth with the sleeve of my dress and told you it was okay—*we're okay* is the mantra of our marriage. But at the station where our train retired and we had to wait for another, I called your older brother and said, "Help."

I don't know why I called. He'd migrated south years ago; there was no help he could offer. There was also no taxi that would take a man stinking wet with vomit. So, I pulled on my big girl panties, tested the muscles in my quads and half-carried you down Park Avenue in Harlem, your feet clumsy but remembering the language of walking. Halfway to the 125th Street subway station, your head slumped to your chest. I could tell it was an act of humiliation more than drunkenness, so I touched your chin and told you to hold that shit up high. *You had a bad night but I fucking love you.* I repeated it over and over, smiling, laughing, because I needed the world to know.

In Harlem, people didn't shun you. They celebrated you; celebrated us.

"That's a wife right there," a man yelled, almost slapping you on the back before catching a whiff and thinking twice.

And I felt proud then, losing my last worries about whether I could get you home to our rundown apartment on the Upper East Side in my high heels and with my broken-jointed toe.

Then came the threat.

A white man on the subway accosted me for bringing you on the nearly empty car, which means he also accosted you, and so I split my throat in two and screamed both a demand and a warning, both a *shut the fuck up* and *if you don't*, sliding up and down on disparate pitches. He was surprised by what he probably perceived as crazy and took off running at the next stop. I ran after him until I remembered your fragile state, braced there against the brown tile wall.

I shook out my wings and took you home.

"I'm okay," you said at our apartment door.

Your body was flooded with apologies then until they were back-logged behind your tongue, but I wish to say now: I never needed them. Not one. I owed you a year of apologies for all the stagnation I'd put you through, the meager freelance paychecks and the not leaving the nest, the crying, the complaints about the noise, the rats, the depression, the waiting for your return. You worked eighty-hour weeks as a resident, night after night of night shift, blood, shit, vomit, drunken patients, patients who thought they could fly, your wolf body shrinking to that of a crow: scraggy and forlorn, hospital scrubs dou-bling as dull feathers, always calling out times of death. No wonder you doused yourself in wine; it is nice not to be nice.

Oh, how we rise and fall in each other's presence.

In Japan, the children are taught *chun chun*. In Turkish, it's *jick jick*. In the future, those whose ears deceive them will simplify my complicated cries about power, love, fence lines, you. Having not learned the language, they'll only bear witness to songs, sometimes serene and lovely enough to open a window to, sometimes brash and loud, a throaty *caw*, reminding them of death and garbage. My voice will be yet another lowly layer of the soundscape—another sound they're unable to decipher or describe and thus just mimic through onomatopoeia.

*Hear this*, they'll say, hoping their children's mouths will form the foreign words. *Hear this*.

- - - - - - - - - - - - - - - - - - - - - - - - - - - - - - - - - - - - - -

PERCEPTION

The term "active listening" is frequently used in the fields of coun-seling, management training, education, and others. It's a technique that requires the listener to concentrate on what's being said. This way, they're able to better comprehend, respond to, and remember what was spoken or signed to them. The listener is also supposed to experience more empathy and understanding, as well as feel more open-minded toward something stated that challenges their worldview.

(Ideally.)

Active listening is also about being open to the possibilities of music, at least according to sound artist Steve Roden. As documented in the 2005 community project "Bronx Soundwalk," people expect to hear music on the radio and in bars or concert halls, but "certainly," as Roden writes, "music is everywhere."

Since we, the active listeners, the perceivers, bring our own meaning to what we hear, Roden argues that we can become "composer listeners." This means deciding what sounds in our environment to listen to and interpret as music, and what sounds to disregard.

People listen to birds chirping and hear music. They stand by the edge of a brook, transfixed by the sound of water flowing over stones, and hear music. Of course, the birds aren't performing arias for a human audience; water isn't chiming to be charming. In reality, the birds are declaring territory and the brook is just following pathways controlled by gravity, elevation, and other earthly forces.

We choose how to perceive our environment.

So, what do we choose to disregard? Given that we live in an era where people still struggle to empathize with each other—instead relying on their prejudices for decision-making—Roden's idea of "composer listeners" can be interpreted through a darker lens. One person hears the coming of change, the other screams too loudly to hear much at all. If you listen to everything, you're left with a harsh, discordant, confusing, and startling symphony.

Perhaps, as humans—these curators of our own perceptions, these "active listeners"—we still always just hear what we want to hear (whether the message is based in love or fear or something else entirely) and ignore the rest.

# The Sound of the Unsaid

It was around one in the morning and a week before the 2016 presidential election when we pulled into the nearly empty parking lot of a gas station in rural Pennsylvania. Kumar killed the engine of the rental car. After getting out and shutting the car door, I whispered, *it's so quiet*, because that's what I always repeated on the handful of times we left New York City during the three years we lived there. *Yeah, it is*, Kumar whispered back. How else does one respond to something so evident?

Kumar jingled the car keys in his hand—a sound that's always reminded me of broken glass—while our two little rescue dogs stared at us with moon eyes from the backseat, silently asking where we were and what was happening. The expanse of darkness beyond the parking lot felt ominous and, above our heads, an overhead lamp crackled, triggering a memory of how papery moths swarmed the porch light of my family's home in Iowa, their bodies creating audible hot vibrations when they flew too close to death.

Now, it was November. There were no insects. I'd like to say I heard the beating wings of an owl or the whip of a bat angling through the air but there was just the crunch of tires over gravel as another vehicle pulled in and parked a few spots away. We locked the car doors and headed inside.

We decided to drive to Kumar's home state of Ohio so he could vote. As a medical student in Boston and then an internal medicine resident in New York City, he hadn't changed his registration. For him, Ohio was still home; our living arrangements had always been temporary. He could have ordered an absentee ballot, but it was a big deal, he said, to vote for the first woman presidential candidate in person. I agreed. We called his parents to let them know we were coming that Friday after he finished work. Kumar rented the car; I packed enough dog food and treats for a week, even though we'd be back by Monday.

Inside the gas station, Kumar grabbed two bottles of water while I roamed the aisles for a snack. I tried to hurry. As we hadn't eaten since lunch though, I couldn't decide what I wanted. "My mom will have food ready for us," Kumar mentioned, but I shot him a look that said, *okay, but I am hungry now*. He wandered away again, knowing not to push too much when my blood sugar is low.

It was while choosing between pretzels and barbecue potato chips that I felt the men closing in.

The signals are often the same: the up-and-down gaze, the *click* of the tongue, the standing too close or not moving to the side, which means, "I own this space," and, by proxy, means, "And therefore I also own you." Or, sometimes, it's just a feeling—a tingle in the gut, a tightening or warming throat. This time, it was the rising hair on my arms.

The pack of white men who followed us into the gas station looked like they were in their mid-twenties, though their faces were lined and worn. One man in an American flag T-shirt watched Kumar reading nutrition labels in the refrigerated aisle. With his hands on his hips, the man flared his nostrils before glancing at his friend in an orange trucker hat. He flicked his chin in Kumar's direction.

The third—a heavy-set man with a shaved head and doughy face stained with dark pink splotches of rosacea—kept his eyes on mine, glaring. My heart raced as if it knew, well before my brain did, that these men wanted my body, our bodies, to be the vessels for their anger and insecurity. I reprimanded myself for taking so long; this was supposed to be a quick stop.

Everything changed in seconds. I snapped my head around to look at Kumar. There he was, examining a cheese stick—a *cheese stick*—while we were being circled like prey. The love I had for him in that moment was overwhelming, as if flowing out of my pores and spilling onto the broken tiled floor. He used a hand to brush away a long strand of hair that covered his eyes.

I yelled the first thing that came to my mind.

THERE'S A MADE-UP word that Kumar and I use with each other: "pockethand." It has literal roots. We were in one of those post-sleeping in Saturday morning moods where everything is funny. Kumar stuck a hand in the deep pocket of my fleece robe, grinned and stated the obvious. Soon, the action or even just the word was used to cheer the other up.

"Pockethand" can be stupid enough to elicit laughter. "Pockethand" is both a noun and a verb. It's also sincere enough to diffuse arguments.

We fight about the normal American things: work stress, unwashed dishes, going for years without taking a vacation, a fear that we'll never pay off our student loans. But tension also arises from outside sources. That's when we attach to one another in solidarity. That's when we "pockethand."

For instance, when white people ask Kumar where he's from, he tells them Kent, Ohio. When they persist, repeating, "Yes, but *where* are you from?" he smiles and says, well, he was born in Lincoln, Nebraska. Is that what they mean?

He's polite but makes them work for it.

When people continue their questioning, and they always do, he relents and tells them that his parents are from India. "I was born in the U.S. though," he clarifies again. They don't care. They have their answer, and never think about why they don't ask other white Americans about where they're from, until they've pushed well past Colorado, Kentucky or Massachusetts and back to their ancestors' homelands. No, he is *the other*, he's been *othered*, and now they try to relate in some way:

"I visited the Taj Mahal once about twenty years ago."
"I've tried Indian food but it's too spicy for me."
"I went on a business trip to Mumbai last year. Great city, but so dirty."

Kumar is gracious about all of this, even though his smile only inflates partway, his eyes focusing not on his inquisitors, but on some distant point. Meanwhile, shame and frustration tighten my throat. As a white kid growing up in Iowa, I maybe would have been ignorant enough to say something similar.

Now, we use "pockethand"—whether it's a whisper or just a quick tug on each other's clothes—as a salve to the slow burn of benevolent racism. *I've got you. I love you. I'm sorry this is happening.* Having the other person's back is vital to any meaningful partnership, of course. But in our marriage, in this era, this pledge increasingly beats with urgency.

Despite the diversity of New York City, people exhale sighs of relief in restaurants and on public transport when they see that Kumar, a bearded brown man, is with me, a white woman. In other areas of the country, men in cars, in stores or on sidewalks watch us, frowning. Once, while shopping at an outlet mall outside of Milwaukee, a man pushed me hard with a shoulder as we strolled by while glaring at Kumar. In this relationship, I'm both a magnet and a shield.

"A patient told me I look like a terrorist," Kumar once texted me from the hospital. "He also told me it's okay though because 'my people' make great doctors."

My fingers fidget over my phone screen, searching for contact, wanting to protect him, to tell him how much I love him, to ask if he's okay. Before any of that, I text: "Pockethand."

We joke about race when we can. Once, while in the shower together, Kumar covered his body in ivory soapsuds, and we pondered what his name would have been if he were a white man. I said "Connor." He said "Chad" and then changed his choice to "Brian." Still, the thirty-something Indian American man passing me the bottle of shampoo is so clearly not a "Brian" that calling him that, even in jest, feels like I'm erasing his identity.

That, and I've heard the stories of others who've tried in seriousness. Back when he still lived in Ohio and went by his first name, Samit, his long-term college girlfriend introduced him to her parents. Her father asked, "Can I call you Sam?" while shaking his hand. Although he had many reasons, this one—this desire of strangers to make his name more palatable to their tongues—was one of his main motivations for showing up at medical school in Boston calling himself by his middle name.

After getting out of the shower, I asked Kumar what "pockethand" means. We'd never actually discussed the definition of it, which, for the first time, struck me as odd. I expected a discussion, or at least his interpretation of it. But without pause, he laughed and yelled: "Pockethand is pockethand!" Then he grinned and wrapped me in hug so tight that I struggled to breathe. I didn't protest though; I just waited until he let me go.

INSIDE THE GAS station in Pennsylvania, I yelled, "I'm going to grab the dogs from the car!"

The men froze.

"What?" Kumar asked. He raised his eyebrows and glanced back at the man in the American flag T-shirt.

"The dogs," I repeated, my hands shaking. "I'm going to let them out."

The men shifted on their feet. Kumar frowned at me again, confused about the dogs—we'd just walked them at the last rest stop—and I put my hand in his coat pocket and pulled him toward the register. I forced myself to stay calm, thinking it'd be worse to panic, to flee outside into the dark. As the cashier yawned and rang up our water and pretzels without looking up from his phone, I talked about how the dogs should go to the bathroom, how excited I was to see his family, about how hungry I was, my mouth just running, running, running, and the men's presence behind us could be felt but the energy had changed.

Their bodies had arrived at the edge. The pressure built. And then the idea of dogs complicating the scene, or just the randomness of the comment, had snapped everyone out of their tension and back into everyday America: we were just milling around in a gas station while country music droned and blistered hot dogs rolled under a heat lamp. Avoiding eye contact, we fast walked to the car. I told Kumar that those men had been close to acting on something. He said that he thought they'd just been watching him like usual, which is why he'd kept his back turned. I said, *no*, it was close, and swung on my seatbelt. Maybe he was right, but my heart was keeping the beat of danger. Our little dogs, that could have been rottweilers or German shepherds for all they knew, wagged their tails in greeting. Kumar drove off.

For the first few minutes afterward, while my adrenaline was wearing off, I felt both like crying and punching the glove box. Worst-case scenarios started playing in my head. I could hear the words. It would be a simple phrase, uttered with malice, like, "Can I help you?" or "Are you from around here?" And because there's no right answer to those questions, because they only seek to instigate, the next words would be uttered far closer to my husband's face, or maybe it'd just be a shove, maybe they'd throw him down, kick him, wait for him to fight back, pull a gun.

On the dark road to Ohio, the gas station now miles behind us, I scanned the tree line for deer, waiting for the flash of a white tail, waiting for impact. Kumar glanced over at me and put his hand on my thigh.

"She'll win," he said.

"What if she doesn't?" I asked. "What if this gets worse?"

He inhaled but didn't have an answer. Instead, he smiled and asked me what he could say to make it better—anything, he'll say it, he just doesn't want to see me so shaken, so concerned for his safety. I shrugged and told him not to worry about it. He is always giving.

After listening to the sounds of the dogs' slow breaths as they fell back asleep, Kumar turned on the radio and adjusted the music to the front speakers only. He was ready to play it loud because loud can be okay too. *No*, can be more than okay—can be a fucking rebellion of sound or a scream of power and persistence. And as he drove, I realized he didn't even have to speak the word or say anything. I didn't need him to. For now, *for now*, we were okay.

- - - - - - - - - - - - - - - - - - - - - - - - - - - - - - - - - - - - - -

RELATIONSHIPS

If two people can be thought of as parallel reflective walls, then a sound that emerges from a place between them would reverberate against their surfaces, remaining stationary in frequency and harmonics. Hear it? Feel it? It's just that same sound bouncing back and forth, back and forth, back and forth. Or, in simpler terms: a flutter echo.

A flutter echo is not well liked by those who deal in sound. Many acoustic experts describe it as energy that's become "trapped." Architects carefully evaluate their designs for flutter echoes, making sure to avoid any unwanted reverberation. Musicians share advice with one another on how to "break up" a flutter echo present in a studio. ("Hang up acoustic panels or foam, use diffusers, add drapes to your windows, place plush furniture in empty spaces . . .")

But perhaps we can rethink how we feel about this shared frequency.

What if it existed for a purpose, whether that purpose be a sign of intimacy, a signal of connection, of shared existence, or just a reminder that everything we do, from clapping our hands to yelling "no!" has a reaction?

Flutter echoes are also commonly recorded as bouncing back and forth up to seven times. Christians, the Jewish people, and naturalists alike might find meaning in this number—after all, the Sabbath is the day God rested, as well as the maximum number for any component in most complex nature-made systems. But regardless of any spiritual or scientific significance, there is something both heartening and forceful about this series of seven echoes. It's a constant underlying connection in the bleakest of worlds—a world without anything there to soften the blow.

*Part*
*Four*

# The Sound of a Poet

On a clear sky morning on Memorial Day in 2018, I made a list of every sound I could hear from the back porch of our little house in the Riverwest neighborhood of Milwaukee. It included the following sounds: my neighbor's brindle-coated pit bull snoring in the grass, the fading bass music of a car several blocks away, a motorcycle backfiring, the Our Lady of Divine Providence's bells ringing out the hour. If I had listened in the early afternoon instead, I maybe would have written down "distant gunshot" right after "the *whirr* of a hummingbird's wings." This is because, that afternoon in a nearby park in Riverwest, a young poet was shot and killed just a few dozen feet away from where children played.

The families enjoying their holiday in the park said on the local evening news that they saw the poet—a twenty-one-year-old man named Juan Bernal—stumble through the grass with his hands behind his head, looking toward the sky. In the game of "guns or fireworks," more than one witness said they'd been hoping that the loud *pop* had been the latter, until they noticed the red stain on his shirt.

He fell near the street and bled to death.

Since reading the book *The Unwanted Sound of Everything* by Garret Keizer last summer, I've been making daily lists of sounds. Keizer recommended the activity—it's an exercise for developing more awareness of the acoustic environment you live in. My lists usually start with the obvious: the garbage truck rumbling through the alley-way, police sirens, cars honking, the church bells, the wind off Lake Michigan rustling the leaves of my neighbor's maple tree, two men on the street cussing at each other, a weed whacker, now a lawnmower, now birds chirping.

The more time I sit on my top wooden stair with a pen and journal, the more human-produced background sounds I notice, like the constant *whoosh* of I-43 traffic or the high-pitched ring emitted from the factory on Gordon Place. Eventually, I feel overwhelmed by the oppressive nature of it. This was the author's point. America's urban dwellers are living in a modern world of *too much sound*, but we've become accustomed to all this noise pollution, just as we've become accustomed to the violence and crime.

According to data collected in 2015 by the FBI Uniform Crime Reporting Program, Milwaukee has the tenth highest murder rate in the country. This means that 24.15 out of 100,000 people were victims of homicide in the span of one year. Roughly 80 percent of those victims were Black men. The number of murders lowered slightly in 2017 but rose again during the COVID-19 pandemic. During the warmer months, I hear gunshots and car tires screeching away from the scene many nights.

I'll admit, at times, I can temporarily forget about Milwaukee's crime statistics, like when I'm running on the Oak Leaf Trail that follows the line of the Milwaukee River, or relaxing on the patio of some local brewery, enjoying the present moment, sip by sip. Other times, just like my reaction to all this noise, I feel like I'm snowed under, even during a Wisconsin summer.

It's not right for me to write about Bernal—I know this. He was Black; I'm white. He grew up with the noise of Milwaukee; I grew up with the sound of my sister's laugh in the flat fields of Iowa. He worked intensely hard to make his own opportunities; as a member of the white middle class, mine were laid out in front of me.

Here's another bit of truth: I didn't know Bernal. As a local writer, I just knew of him.

Yet, in the vibrant, violent, diverse, beautiful, too-loud city of Milwaukee, I simply wish to write that one noise that shouldn't have been lost from this soundscape is this person's voice. Even though he was only a couple of years out of high school, Bernal gave poetry workshops to groups of children and adults around town. He graced open mics throughout Milwaukee and recited his work. He rapped. He spoke. He incited snaps and tears and applause. And when local teachers, artists, friends, and family members wrote or talked about Bernal after his death, they all used words like "inspiration," "joy," and "potential."

People say the same thing about Milwaukee: it has potential. If only it could overcome its decades of racism, redlining, oppression, and crime.

From the same book that recommended recording a list of sounds, I learned that the modern world has become so loud that millions of people suffer hearing loss due to all the noise. Researchers in Sweden found that the chronic sound of distant traffic raises the rate of depression. In Japan, researchers reported that you're more likely to experience hypertension, which can lead to heart disease, if you live near a highway. The number of hours of sleep lost to exhaust pipes, honking horns, overhead airplanes, and hissing factories are so massive that its effects are unable to be tracked.

The noise is killing us, it seems.

Yet, in response to the question of, "How bad?" the blue collar, no collar, fighting-for-life people of Milwaukee may list the wolf at the door well before noting the late-night group of Harleys cruising the streets. In a city of segregated lines, there's a lot more than noise doing the killing.

Last year, I visited the spot in Kern Park where Bernal was murdered and recorded a list of sounds. The loudest noise was the passing speeding traffic on Humboldt Street but there was also birdsong, the drowsy buzz of insects, and the laughter of children chasing each other around a thick stand of pine trees. When I stood in front of Bernal's makeshift memorial though all I could think about was silence.

"What an incredible loss," I say to other Milwaukee writers when we talk about him, as if that helps, as if that even remotely conveys what people directly affected by his absence feel.

Once, in an anechoic chamber at a sound lab in Minneapolis, I heard the rush of my own pulsing blood inside my neck. I wonder if that's what people hear right before death—if their senses get stripped back raw and now the once barely audible is all amplified: robins pecking for worms in the soil (they first cock their heads and listen for movement); the soft clattering of oak leaves, rustled by the breeze. Meaning, is all this noise vivid and decipherable in just one quick moment, right before it stops?

I can only fathom whether this is true, but what I have witnessed are the aftershocks of Bernal's death still reverberating around Milwaukee. In a comment made on an online post about the poet's death, a man wrote, "My god, I just heard you read last month." Amongst all the shock and grief and horror, this comment triggered one heartening thought within me: his voice.

It was forever recorded in yet another person's list of sounds.

- - - - - - - - - - - - - - - - - - - - - - - - - - - - - - - - - - - - - - - - - - -

### VIOLENCE

For those who didn't grow up with exposure to firearms, "guns or fireworks?" is a common quandary. The sound of fireworks shares enough similarities with the sound of gunshots that many nearby listeners may become momentarily uneasy, even on a day when fireworks are common, such as the Fourth of July or New Year's Eve. So, to dispel any confusion, here is quick guide on how to decipher between the two:

1. Although the levels of flash powder allowed in consumer fireworks are monitored in the states where they're legal to sell, fireworks can still produce a loud and startling "pop." That explosion often produces a noise as high as 150 decibels or more—a level known to cause permanent hearing damage.
2. Generally, though, fireworks produce a much lower energy "pop" than guns. Furthermore, the noise of, say, a red, white, and blue comet-tailed Roman Candle, is often followed by a whistling or crackling "whiz."

3. For comparison, the report or muzzle blast of a gun—which refers to when the gas is released from the barrel—is different than that "pop" of fireworks. It produces a booming "crack" or "snap" that, at anywhere from 110 to 175 decibels, is loud enough to echo throughout a gun range, a field, a neighborhood . . .

4. . . . a shopping mall, a church, a college campus, a night club, a bar, a concert venue, a movie theatre, a Walmart, a grocery store, an office, a spa . . .

5. . . . a school . . .

6. The other sound a gun can make is a high-pitched "buzz," which may remind you of an angry bee. This is the sound of a lead bullet traveling over eighteen hundred miles per hour through the air, faster than the speed of sound. If you hear this noise zipping overhead or near your ear, you are very likely in trouble.

7. In this case, immediately follow the direction that every child in America now understands: drop and find cover.

# The Sound of a Shot Spotted

She panicked a few seconds after the first fireworks exploded.

Launched near Lake Michigan, copper stars and willow trees made of gunpowder crackled in the sky over our old Polish neighborhood of Riverwest in Milwaukee. It was a mistake to keep the back door open, to not usher our smallest dog to safety inside. We didn't know how loud the celebrations would be from our house; Kumar and I had only moved from New York City a month ago.

After tearing away from the porch, she found refuge under the bed upstairs. We got on our knees and tried to coax her out. We said, we're sorry, sweetie. We said, it's okay. You're okay. But her fear of loud noises was born, or maybe an internal locket holding terror—quivering in her chest since puppyhood—was opened.

Fireworks, thunder, gunshots, she tucked her tail and cowered as if expecting sound to be solidified into fists. From then on, when the sun set and the neighborhood became purse-clutching dark, became watch-your-back blind corners and simmering summer alleyways, we worried that her little terrier heart would explode from all that fear triggered by the loud noises that were so frequent and so close.

On nights she cowered in the closet, I placed my hands on the soft fur of her deep wrestler chest and told her *no* in a mother's voice—calm, quiet, assertive. Her flesh vibrated against my palms. After a few minutes, she stopped shaking and I rolled her over and rubbed her pink drum-tight belly. Her front paws went limp at their lowest joint, like two broken daffodils, and her eyes lost that wild look. But her world was no longer smells, the way it should be with dogs. It was just ears pricked and alert, waiting for impending doom in the form of vibrations cracking the quiet.

SOME DAYS, I want to curl in on myself, grow a shell, a shield. I can breathe through occasional fireworks. Thunder shushes the earth and calms my thinking; even birds close their beaks. But in response to gunshots, my heart goes feral. Both of our dogs—the one who fears noise and the one who doesn't—must sense my hypocrisy. The sudden surplus of adrenaline sends a jolt of tingles down my spine and my gut drops like I'm in a car speeding over the apex of a hill. I only pretend to be calm.

Some locals refer to this type of reaction as "weakness." In Milwaukee, one's cocky apathy for violence and all the noise it creates is an admirable trait. Chaos is treated as a norm, not a situation that can be—should be—prevented. The Rust Belt's dismissive attitude is pervasive. *Relax!* people say. Grab another beer. Get over it. Toughen up.

On my neighborhood's Facebook page, residents post concerns about all the muggings, car thefts, high-speed chases, break-ins, and more.

"Two young men robbed me at gunpoint last night," one neighbor writes.

"Has anyone seen this car? It was stolen out of my garage."

"Heads up, there are five men casing houses on Booth."

"Fam, don't go to this bar. It's full of racists."

"Were those fireworks or gunshots?"

"I don't feel safe leaving the house."

"Help."

To all of this, people write comments like, "If you can't handle it then move to Mequon." Mequon is a quiet, safe, wealthy suburb north of the city.

As an outsider, it's difficult to comprehend this mindset. We don't just *exist* in our new environment. Kumar and I don't fill our days reacting to incidents seemingly out of our control. We plan. We seek change. Our privilege is the privilege to look ahead, to want more and know how to get it, to be equipped to get it. Our privilege is my whiteness. His education. Our jobs. After all these years, I swear I can hear success. It sounds like wind rustling through bluestem prairies and pine trees. It sounds like quiet. First, though, it sounds like the realtor hammering the For Sale sign into our front garden.

Some people here feel the way same way; others don't.

For now, I can stand the aural output of Milwaukee's high rates of violent crime, but I refuse to become accustomed to it. Our heads swivel toward the *pop pop pop*, instinctually searching for the source, but afterward Kumar and I compare notes and find that the echoes and walls and wind have us all confused. Shots come from two or three blocks north, or maybe it was west, or southwest. We don't know.

The terrier doesn't care about the logistics. She's just gone. Only the trigger puller, still-conscious victim, or witness can say, *right here*.

Or so I thought.

Now, computer screens show a dot on a map where the sensors calculated that a shooting took place. The police drive to the location and search the ground for shells, casings, blood, and bodies, without anyone on the ground necessarily ever reporting so much as a whimper.

OUR TERRIER ISN'T the only one listening for death. Across Milwaukee, acoustic sensors are attached to electricity poles and stoplights. Precise locations aren't always disclosed, but the sensors—which contain a microphone, GPS, cell capability, memory, and processing—are installed in the city's most violent neighborhoods. They're there to detect and record gunfire. Unlike humans, the recordings relay the evidence without shock or confusion.

The program responsible for the sensors is called ShotSpotter. Cities across the U.S. have purchased it for their police departments. In Oakland, Miami, Cincinnati, New Haven, Baltimore, and Chicago, gunfire is no longer just heard on the streets. Previously, someone could shoot a gun and the only way law enforcement would know is if someone called 911, yelling, *two blocks north, maybe west*. Now, we are creating an acoustic record of our country's violence.

This is how it works: computers use a system of audio triangulation based on the volume of the gunshot and how long it takes to travel to each sensor. After using sound-analyzing algorithms, the system can pinpoint where the noise occurred almost instantly.

These recorded clips of gunshots—or something close to them, like firecrackers or a car backfiring—are then transmitted to a review center. There, humans do what computers still cannot: listen to and flesh out the possible scene with detail for the police. If an acoustic expert confirms the noise was a gunshot, notifications are sent to police dispatch centers, patrol cars, and officers' phones. ShotSpotter informs them of the sounds of multiple shooters; they report the possibility of an automatic weapon. Even without hearing the gunfire, law enforcement has an idea of what to expect upon arriving at the scene. All of this—the sensors, the triangulated location, the analyzing of the acoustics, the alerts to police—is completed within a minute or less.

But.

While the idea may be good ...

The reality is that Milwaukee spends around $450,000 a year for ShotSpotter's services for coverage of twelve square miles of the city. This doesn't include the hefty installation and startup costs. And the statistics on ShotSpotter's success rates are, well, spotty. For instance, in 2016, the city of San Antonio spent about $546,000 total on the program. The results? Local police made four arrests in one year based on ShotSpotter's services. This makes the sum of one arrest more than $136,500.

In Milwaukee—five years after the system was installed and one year after it was expanded—ShotSpotter and the Milwaukee Police Department reported that during a nine-month period, 10,285 alerts about shots fired led to only 172 arrests.

Why so few arrests? Most of the time, the police pull up at an empty corner after receiving an alert. They may be aware of the gunfire now, yes, but who sticks around to be handcuffed—or killed by police—after pulling the trigger?

What the technology also lacks is the ability to measure the acoustic waves hitting each nearby resident. Sometimes I feel like Milwaukee has sunk into Wisconsin's marshy mud water, or like Lake Michigan breached its banks, and the *booms* and *bangs* keep breaking the stillness like thrown stones. We are all living in the water and the ripples may never stop.

"I THINK SHE's getting better," Kumar said two weeks after the Fourth of July.

We were walking on the trail that follows the east side of the Milwaukee River, which is bordered on either side by tall grass. Both dogs had inflated with pride and purpose, like mini fox-tailed soldiers. Their legs seemed propelled by joy.

"She's always fine in nature," I said. "She's always fine where it's quiet."

We passed a large tree that had been severed near the base of its trunk where a beaver had gnawed through the wood. The dogs paused, sniffing at the crime scene, and then marked the felled tree with urine. Up ahead, a factory hissed steam. Seagulls squawked as they clustered in the air above a stretch of rapids, hunting for fish.

These walks lower our stress. Before moving to Milwaukee, Kumar and I rescued our two small dogs not just out of a need for companionship, but also as a way of staying sane. The city was too loud. The only people evading the noise pollution were our coworkers, the ones with cars and family vacation homes in the Catskills or on Long Island, the ones with enough money to leave.

One dog was lost but confident; the other—the terrier—was broken and deeply insecure. We rehabilitated them both, spending hours in the calmest, least traversed sections of Central Park and Randall's Island, or along the East River. They both learned to tolerate living in an unnatural environment. But I didn't. My ears needed an escape valve. So, when Kumar matched for a gastroenterology fellowship at a hospital in Milwaukee, we thought this place would be a sanctuary in comparison to the last three years we'd spent on a loud, congested island.

In many ways, it is. We have river trails, access to open green space, a tiny backyard with birds and tomato plants, lake waves that are far louder than Lakeshore Drive's traffic, freedom to travel. We have a significantly reduced amount of noise pollution, which means I don't feel so trapped anymore. *I'm okay.* But vehicles screech past our house at high speeds, keeping ahead of the sirens, maybe slamming into a parked car along the way—an audible reminder that we will have to wait for peace. Gunshots go off but the acoustic sensors don't pick up on shaking hands or a little dog jammed underneath the bed. Our bodies hear the violence even if we try to train our ears to ignore it.

We hope that our smallest dog won't regress any further. I don't know if she can learn to tolerate the sounds of small explosions; I just know she shouldn't have to.

WHY AM I writing about *she*: a dog?

My god. *She*: a girl. *They*: children.

On November 19, 2018, a thirteen-year-old girl named Sandra Parks was killed in her home on the north side of Milwaukee, a mile and a half from our house. She became the seventh child to die from stray bullets or crossfire in this city since 2014. The year before her death, she won third place in her age group for the city's Martin Luther King Jr. writing contest. Her essay pleads for an end to gun violence and then provides a message of hope and faith. *Milwaukee Magazine* published it posthumously. In the first paragraph, she wrote:

> I put my headphones on and let the music take me away. I move to the beat and try to think about life and what everything means. When I do, I come to the same conclusion . . . we are in a state of chaos. In the city in which I live, I hear and see examples of chaos almost everyday. Little children are victims of senseless gun violence.

Parks used the term "hear and see," not the more traditional order of "see and hear." She was perceptive; she knew her world. Quiet comes with a price tag that only the privileged can afford. Her essay focused on Milwaukee's poor Black neighborhoods, redlined, gutted, and cut through with Interstate 43, separated from the lake, the river, from lead-free water, from funding and jobs, from good schools, from, at the very least, *decent* and *functioning* schools. These are the streets where the acoustic sensors are placed.

That night, a bullet intended for another body came through Parks' bedroom window, hitting her in the chest. Her family described her demeanor as "calm." Her sister said she reacted to the trauma "like a soldier." Her mother used the word "angel." She was declared dead soon after she arrived at the hospital.

*It's okay.* The shot was spotted but not seen.

*You're okay.* The sensors only recorded the sound of the bullet as it left the gun.

*We're sorry.* We are all working on a shell, a shield.

This city needed that girl; this city killed her. She had a right to life regardless of who she was or would become. Here, *hear*, lies the apathy: the acoustic sensors record without stopping. Allow me the homophone. Whatever happens, there is no moment of silence. No respect for a family's grief. No end. Who knows whether an alert was sent or whether it would have made a difference?

*Fact*: We are paying for others to listen to our chaos and report back to us on how we're failing.

IN 2014 THE *New Yorker* published a poem by the poet and writer Ocean Vuong called "Someday I'll Love Ocean Vuong." Recently, upon revisiting this poem, I paused at this line: "Don't be afraid, the gunfire is only the sound of people trying to live a little longer." I read it again, then recited it out loud.

ShotSpotter is based in California. Meaning, the city of Milwaukee pays for the company's out-of-state employees to monitor the sounds of the still-recovering Rust Belt, including the all-day and night fireworks on the Fourth of July. Guns/fireworks: look at our terrier's tucked tail. The quality of sound is almost the same. Each *boom* and *bang* would have triggered an alert to their system's computers, and while sitting at work with a pair of headphones on, maybe experiencing the beginning tinges of a headache, acoustic experts in Silicon Valley would have evaluated thousands of those false alarms to decide whether it was the product of a bullet.

The exercise seems inane. If the limited, well-protected ShotSpotter data is correct, then one could extrapolate that we could do better at keeping people alive. We could provide people with thousands of other options for how to live a life. To thrive. It's far easier to install microphones than to fund schools, to stop evictions, to provide resources, to undo what's been done.

We'd come to perceive Milwaukee's tolerance of crime to be apathy. Toughness. But of course, that isn't the full story. "Move to the suburbs" is a shitty response to a person in crisis but learning not to hide from the gunshots is also a form of survival. It's a form of moving forward, of self-soothing, an insight into what it takes to start pulling the trigger, an answer to the why, a *been here long enough* to know things won't change because this town won't do what's necessary to change them.

*We're sorry*—even if it is eventually stated—will never be enough.

WHO ELSE IS listening? I recently read in *Smithsonian Magazine* and *Scientific American* that environmental scientists have discovered that plants are capable of sensing sound. Studies showed that some flowers—such as the *oenothera drummondii*, or beach evening primrose—produced more nectar or released more pollen when exposed to the sound of bee wings. And pea seedlings grew in the direction of the sound of water flowing through a pipe, even though they still tunneled through dry dirt.

Perhaps, in the past, we've underestimated plants' responses to sound because we can't perceive them in the same way we can in animals or other humans. Nature is often described as apathetic. Surroundings can't be controlled; rooted things can't run or fly away. But along the Milwaukee River, the sound of the relentless gnawing of beaver teeth creates a current of invisible acoustic waves—each rapid a vibration that breaches the tree bark, flooding the molecules and cells that comprise the wood. I wonder if the leaves shudder. I wonder if they feel the fear.

Sandra Parks wrote, *I hear and see examples of chaos almost everyday.* Our dog is now hiding behind a pile of sweaters in the closet. My heart is pounding. I yell Kumar's name from the top of the stairs. And we're the ones who have it good. We have it so good. But it's not just ShotSpotter's sensors monitoring this world we created: if nature is listening for life, perhaps it is also listening for death. There's a lesson there, the way it endures despite such closeness.

- - - - - - - - - - - - - - - - - - - - - - - - - - - - - - - - - - - - - - - - -

## LINES

Segregation is often discussed regarding its effects on education, employment, housing, crime, police brutality, access to healthy food, access to healthcare, access to green space, to clean water, to clean air, to safe places to walk or bike or watch your kids play. Yet, as detailed in a 2017 study from some of the nation's top environmental health researchers, there's also a strong correlation between noise pollution and poor minority neighborhoods in segregated cities.

By linking a map of sound measurements to U.S. demographics data, the researchers found that affluent communities, whether in the country or city, were much quieter. In fact, communities with median annual incomes below $25,000 were, on average, two decibels louder than areas where residents pulled in $100,000 a year or more. (For context, our ears usually perceive an increase of ten decibels as "doubling" the noise.) Furthermore, neighborhoods with predominantly Black residents were found to have the highest median noise levels at night.

So why are marginalized neighborhoods louder? Oppression, less political power, and limited economic clout have all resulted in a decrease in enforcement of noise regulations, as well as limited involvement in land use decisions. This comes at a cost to residents. Think: interstates and highways cutting through and destroying main streets, community centers, and houses in Black neighborhoods. Think: industrial facilities and airports. Think: a forced tolerance of noise instead of the privilege to enjoy quiet streets, quiet cars, quiet appliances, and access to nature.

This link between noise pollution and social factors is far-reaching. For instance, the noisiest city in the world—Mumbai, India—has a chasm between the impoverished and affluent that can be both seen and heard. Measuring at 95.3 decibels in some areas during the day, Mumbai suffers from train and traffic noise, industrial noise and music played over loudspeakers. Only a small percentage of the city's approximately 20 million residents can find relief from the noise in the form of high-rise buildings in wealthy neighborhoods.

Yet, the problem isn't just the irritating presence of noise, like it's a barking dog or a high school garage band. Exposure to chronic noise pollution triggers the release of stress hormones, which, over time, can increase residents' heart rates and blood pressure. This can lead to type 2 diabetes, cardiovascular disease, and lower birth weight. Consequences also include poor sleep and mental health issues.

All of this is to say that peace and quiet and, by association, a better quality of life, are privileges that go to the highest bidder.

# The Sound of a Slow Bleed

First, we used the term "needs space." My sister needed space because she was figuring things out, going through something—what was the other word?—coping. Next, we said that my sister needed time to heal. Healing is different than coping. It takes longer, apparently, and seeing as it'd been three months since she'd picked up the phone or responded to a text or letter or allowed my parents to see their grandchildren, clearly, she was healing.

Another few months of silence passed and any time my mother or father said, "healing," I thought of a fractured bone—that sliver of vulnerability shooting across a slab of white rock. I didn't understand how something so rigid is supposed to meld back together. More weeks went by and for some reason, "heal" now made me conjure a more serious medical condition: a ruptured appendix. If you survive it, the recovery is extensive.

When I was in high school, the news story I read about a girl who died of a ruptured appendix had, in my mind, experienced an internal explosion, like her appendix—this fragile, taut balloon of an organ—had just gone *pop!* in her belly. It wasn't until my early twenties that I learned that the condition begins with a tear, maybe no longer than a centimeter, but that tiny rip—as innocuous as a split seam on a teddy bear—allows for the contents to leak. Slowly, slowly, there goes the polyester filling, there goes the sheep's wool, the fluffy cotton and childhood memories, or any memory in which we loved her, which was all of them, lost into the cavernous spaces of the abdomen.

This analogy works in a different way. The leak poisons the body and tells my sister not to come back, even when my eight-year-old niece—her eldest daughter—calls me from her bedroom, maybe from the bunk bed she shares with her younger sister. She didn't ask me questions, but rather just waited to be asked how she was and what she was doing. As I inquired how soccer practice was going, I was uncertain whether she even played. I do not pretend to be a good aunt. But she was young enough, kind enough, not to judge.

Before we hung up, her father, my sister's husband, entered her bedroom, thus hearing my final question: Do you ever call your grandparents anymore? She told me she wasn't allowed. Because her father overheard the end of our clandestine conversation, we're forbidden from ever speaking without his monitoring. We don't speak again.

A full year goes by, including all its holidays, birthdays, and anniversaries. No one is dealing well, but now we're using the term "banished." My sister banished us from her life. Is that the right word? We get mixed up with the verb and subject; did she exile herself or evict us? Although we both distanced ourselves from our father—at least temporarily—it feels unnatural for a child to outright abandon their parents, especially the ones who helped raise her four children, the ones who picked up the phone, who wrote checks and insisted on college, the ones who were imperfect but trying, who—yes—insisted on a tense Midwestern quiet when maybe they should have encouraged sound. Still.

They love her. They love their grandchildren. "Imagine how big they must be," they say every time I visit or call.

I have two dogs that my parents now receive photos of over text message. A husband. Having children enters my mind, once, twice, then dozens of times, but I cannot replace flesh and souls with other flesh and souls. There is no trade—no body for a body. They would only be lacking, just as I am lacking, just as I am unable to fill this hole.

This *estrangement*.

My mother first used the word at Christmas. Before, in my twenties, I skipped most of the holidays, blamed my inability to fly home on my bank account, which was half true. When they offered to buy me a ticket, I blamed it on my first dog. The dying dog. I couldn't just leave him with a dog sitter. He needed me. (I needed him.) In reality, I was just trying to figure out who I was outside of my family. But total absolute silence from a daughter is something new for my parents. It's permanent. Solid. Without stated reason. It's hitting hard, hitting heavy.

For me, my sister's estrangement has been a slow leak. I can point to the rupture; I often do in essays. She comes home from a weekend Evangelical Christian camp for young teens, I'm standing there by the piano, she's lifting her arms, her eyes are different, she's different. Booklets damning me to hell appear, warning me to accept or else.

Here's something I'd forgotten: When my parents first confronted her on her newfound zealot status, she fled the house. Charged with the mission of locating their missing middle schooler, I'd donned my hiking boots and wrapped a red bandana around my forehead— I'd been expecting a long and intrepid search. I was disappointed to spot her figure from the sidewalk; she was crouched in-between two arborvitaes in the next door neighbor's front yard. I lingered. She knew I could see her. I told her that mom and dad were worried. Stop hiding. Come home.

Even after wrestling her way out of the shrubbery, she didn't look me in the eyes. That night, she raised her hands into the air again, praising Jesus. The leak widened into a hemorrhage.

This is the difference between siblings and parents. For all these years, I've committed myself to self-preservation and watched my sister from afar, choosing to stay quiet—you know by now that I can be *so quiet*. My parents accepted her changed nature; they let it wash over them like baptismal water, because what was the other choice? Abandon their child? Replace her high-pitched laugh with the polite clink of silverware, with cleared throats and closed mouth chewing, with only a TV to mask the sound of what's missing? Other parents lose their children's voices in an instant—their words are ripped from their mouth by uncontrollable forces, by internal explosions, their lives just go *pop!* and everyone sits in the silence, in the wake, waiting for the return of a breath that just won't come.

For my parents, my sister, me, it's still possible. Sometimes I want to scream that we can cauterize it. Stitch it up. Stop it. I don't care what the analogy is; this is the sound of a slow bleed, not a death.

Still, three years later and my mother is on the living room couch, her lips once again forming the word "estranged," so cautious, so fearful, like it's some consonant-clogged foreign word that her tongue cannot master. But I see the understanding in her face. Forever is a word my family uses now too although—*listen*—we still raise the pitch at the end: a question mark.

- - - - - - - - - - - - - - - - - - - - - - - - - - - - - - - - - - - - - - - - - - - - -

## ABSENCE

As described by Michel Chion in his book *Sound*, we often become much more aware of a noise after its cessation. We only notice things once they're gone, like the click of the dog's nails on the wooden floor after he passes away, for instance. (He always rushed toward the door to greet you.) Without that click, the room pulses with an unfamiliar and mournful quiet.

Maybe these acoustic memories can be described as "ghost sounds."

Simultaneously, the dying down of a certain sound can reveal a masked sound, a hidden noise that was always present but inaudible to a listener's ears until this moment. The hum of the refrigerator becomes prominent at night after you turn off the radio. The song of crickets seems to ratchet up in volume after the crackling campfire dies down. The absence of a laugh leaves an awkward quiet in its wake.

This sentiment is perhaps better expressed through poetry. The fifteenth- and sixteenth-century Japanese haiku artist Ikenishi Gonsui wrote the following poem:

The raw winter wind
Has died down leaving only
The sound of the sea

And here's another haiku from the Edo period poet Bashō. It also takes place in the season of loss, which makes sense; there is grief in this idea of aural absence:

Awake at night—
The sound of the water jar
Cracking in the cold

Of course, only the first poem explicitly mentions the dying down of one sound, leaving another one exposed. But we can assume that because of nighttime's quiet (or the dearth of daytime's noise), your ears would perk at the sound of the jar fracturing, of the water freezing and expanding, of your whole world splitting and fracturing—

—and wait for the inevitable next noise of everything falling apart.

# The Sound of Morning Quiet

*Possibility 1*

The dogs and I are out for a walk on the Milwaukee River trail on this late November morning. In the woods, near the underside of the North Avenue Bridge, we pass a structure constructed from large tree branches all stood upright and leaned together, resembling a dilapidated teepee. Trash circles the makeshift campsite—crushed Miller Lite cans, cigarettes butts, soiled clothing, an empty bag of off-brand potato chips.

We passed this spot thirty minutes earlier on our route and, at the time, there was—and maybe still is—somebody inside. Still, the dogs and I walk by on the way back and witness no one. Nothing. Whoever's inside stays inside. We go home.

*Possibility 2*

The dogs and I are out for a walk on the Milwaukee River trail on this late November morning. My breath turns to steam against my wool scarf. We left the house before dawn, using the back gate that leads to the alleyway. Our neighborhood, Riverwest, is comprised of Polish Flats built in 1900 or shortly before. Overhead are low-strung electric wires and seagulls escaping the pummeling winds off Lake Michigan. All these working-class houses and their little yards lie in the shadow of the Our Lady of Divine Providence cathedral, which has a steeple bell that rings every hour and half hour, forever marking time, even when you're trying to sleep.

I like this place, its people, and their dedication to never backing down, but only when it's quiet. Morning quiet. Gentle quiet. Nighttime quiet is different—it beats in your throat like a threat, saying *watch your back*. Word travels over our chain-link fences: my neighbors get held up at gunpoint, lose their wallets, their purses, their children's backpacks, their cars.

I tell them my own stories: a description of the blue Hyundai that followed me, the man inside of it, masturbating. The aggressive pit bull in the yard next to the daycare. *It jumped the fence?* They ask. *Yes,* I say, it jumped the fence. The baby I cradled near a t-boned car while his mother asked the police how she could possibly afford insurance. Like, where do you think we are? I tell my neighbors about the young boy lying motionless on the sidewalk with blood streaming out of his mouth, struck by a van while crossing the street at the corner, half a block from the elementary school. His older sister was screaming, pulling her own hair out, and I said, *it's okay, he will be okay,* and she gave me the look I deserved—a look that said, *no, he will not.*

My license plates? Removed with a wrench. My car windows? Smashed. Me too, they say. Us too. We also talk about cars that aren't our own. The silver sports car that ran a red light when he saw me and my dogs in the crosswalk, sped up to over 70 mph in a 25-mph zone and—as we were head down, minds blank sprinting for our lives to the curb—flew by, just a couple inches from our bodies.

*Do you think? He was trying? To kill you?* They ask.

Yes, but why?

There is a lot to say about the cars here. Drivers travel at drunken speeds and crash into each other, or into stop signs, fire hydrants, trees and houses. I hear the screech of rubber tires on cement, then the impact, then the yelling and cursing. Once, a man in a suv being chased by another man in a pick-up truck created a perfect square of destruction around our house: two cars were hit one block southeast, a station wagon and truck were flipped over one block west, a city bus was struck one block northwest and—for the final act—two more cars were totaled one block north before both suv and truck lost control and landed tires up. Both men fled the scene on broken legs. Did they ever catch them? We don't know.

Still.

*Still.*

I like the mornings because there's no chaos. If there are sirens, they're from ambulances picking up the bodies of addicts who died the night before. This city has sunk me down deep into selfishness. Before getting involved, I ask myself, will this situation endanger a child, a woman, an innocent bystander, my husband, my dogs, me? No? Then I walk on by. I have walked by two of the dead, both times men, feet or hands sticking out from under white sheets, feeling nothing but numb. When I shake my head and look solemn, I do it for show.

This cold November morning, there are no sirens. No warnings. The dogs trot next to each other, almost step for step. Like all well-treated dogs, they're excited just to be alive.

We pass the factory on Gordon Place that pumps out metallic smelling smoke and then turn south onto the bike trail that follows the line of the Milwaukee River, with woods on either side. Ten minutes later, we reach the pedestrian bridge that crosses the river. The temperature drops as we walk over the water; cold rapids churn toward Lake Michigan, which is less than a mile away as the crow flies. That chilled air reminds me of the void.

After crossing the bridge, you can choose to either go up the stairs that lead toward Milwaukee's Lower East Side, descend to an outcropping littered with used needles and fishing lures, or go north along the gravel nature trail that follows the east side of the river.

This morning, instead of heading down the river trail by the broken structure, I change my planned route and walk the dogs up toward the Lower East Side's cream brick houses and, eventually, the lakeshore. Safe.

*Possibility 3*

The dogs and I are out for a walk on the Milwaukee River trail on this late November morning. The static *ring* of the frothing, icy water doesn't warn me; I go north down the river trail. I unhook the dogs' leashes from their collars and wait near the graffiti-covered ruins of a concrete retaining wall. They sniff and pee. The sun is up but the haze hasn't lifted. After *clicking* my tongue, the dogs sprint toward me and I watch their muscular little bodies. I wonder what it'd be like to fly across dirt like that on rabbit-size paws. They race in front of me down the trail and so I yell, *heel!* and they do.

We amble past the broken structure that sometimes shelters unhoused men and I note the signs of human life around it. My head goes left-right, left-right, always watching for a man, for men, for the source of the *pop pop pop*—why do men always shoot at least three bullets? A man on a mountain bike in full athletic gear approaches us and my breathing slows: early-to-rise men in chrome sunglasses and spandex shorts are usually obsessed with their own fitness and adrenaline, nothing more.

The steam from another factory hisses. The dogs and I stroll through a cemetery of scrub trees felled by beavers and mounds of drooping yellow grass, buried under frost. In the summertime, the land that slopes down toward the riverbank is littered with wildflowers. The seedlings bake in the sun and bloom into daisies, golden alexanders, wild geraniums, and mayapples. Yet, in November, the brown water slides by stony hibernating earth. The river's usually wide borders have also slimmed before the first Wisconsin snowfall. It will all be frozen soon.

I stop my *move forward* mentality to let the dogs play in an open area in the woods. My smaller dog unfurls her curly tail until it almost touches the ground and uses it like a rudder for maximum control as she zooms past obstacles at hyper speed. The other dog leaps onto a fallen tree to escape her crazy.

I think, *this is perfect, this is enough*, and cut the walk short by way of Locust Street Bridge. The traffic has picked up and I don't like the bone-crushing height of this bridge, but by the time we reach the open space of Gordon Park on the west side—our side—the dogs' tails are swinging, and we're headed home for breakfast.

*Possibility 4*

The dogs and I are out for a walk on the Milwaukee River trail on this late November morning. I loosen the scarf wrapped around my face as my muscles warm from exercise. Why would I cross a busy bridge to go back to the west side when I could just backtrack on the river trail and use the pedestrian bridge? Why would I not extend this walk by a mile because all my dogs want to do is run? Be in nature? Rejoice? They gaze up at me with those dark brown eyes and I remember, *oh yeah*, we're okay. An elderly woman with a stiff-jointed Great Dane passes us, smiling. A young man with a backpack stops and stares at a cellphone screen, his thumbs a blur, going *beep boop beep*. An irritated, unseen owner calls a Golden Retriever, black with river mud, back into the woods. We are fine.

But as we meander back south, we're alone again. My head isn't clear either; I'm indulging in a fantasy in which we live in an old house on the coast that is surrounded by fields and trees and a feeling of freedom, like I could just lie down and close my eyes without worrying about what will happen to my body. The smell of salt is in the air. Blue sky. The dogs roam near this big, safe house. My sister is there. Maybe a baby: mine. It's quiet except for a sharp breeze rattling the skeletons of shrubs. I imagine the first flakes of snow falling. Meaning, I'm not even dreaming of spring. Milwaukee weather isn't what makes me go to the imaginary.

I'm watching my dogs both in real time and in my mind. In my mind, they can expand their reaches because I'm not controlling them with this invisible lever of fear. I'm not calling them back to a position by my feet. I'm also not touching the cold metal of the folded tactical knife in my left coat pocket, head going left-right, left-right.

*Possibility 5*

The dogs and I are out for a walk on the Milwaukee River trail on this late November morning and we've reached this point, the only possibility left. The structure near the underside of the North Avenue Bridge simmers with bad energy. If you prefer to stay above ground, avoid places that block the view of the sky. Underneath the sleeves of my sweater, the hair on my arms rises. The dogs smooth their ears back into submission and fall behind me without being told to; we are little fish moving through big currents.

My eyes scan for movement. I spot a pair of busted shoes and a red T-shirt strewn in the grass. Nothing more. Until I see the man. A tall, heavily built white man sitting on the trunk of a fallen tree next to the structure, dressed in navy blue sweatpants and a black sweatshirt with the hood up. Brown boots. His elbows rest on his knees; his hands obscure most of his face. And next to his thigh, the blade of a ten-inch knife is stuck into the wood.

The dim sunlight provides the action I was searching for: rays reflect off the steel, shifting the light. Adrenaline clutches my throat and travels up into my mouth, my cheeks, my nose. The man jolts his head up. His face is all pain and hatred as he wraps his fingers around the handle of the knife.

*Possibility 6*

~~The dogs and I are out for a walk on the Milwaukee River trail on this late November morning.~~ Here we are. The end. I see it all: *I'm outsized in knife and strength. I run. No, I fight. But whichever one I choose I scream until my voice breaks and my little dogs are a flurry of wrath and teeth. After that knife goes in my neck or chest—it just takes one good stab, although in my imagination the coroner will say it was over twenty, no, thirty wounds—and I'll go down, and then get up, repeat, repeat, and then go down for good. There is too much blood. The dogs, I hope, will leave me.*

I remember to breathe. The man hasn't moved but his body is tight, at the brink, ready to unload, watching me. I'm not even resisting an urge to run—right now my job is to pass by this broken human holding a massive knife as if it's *no big deal.* Eyes forward, head up, shoulders back, hands in pockets, relaxed. Look how cool I am.

I even sniff the way men sniff and crinkle their noses, narrow their eyes and consider the ground. Unhappy but in control. Life sucks but what are you going to do? There is something powerful about that quick, loud inhalation of air. If this man wants to murder me then he'd be murdering a comrade, another person who gets it, another Milwaukeean, not just a woman. Right? Look at the way I'm mimicking your behavior. We are in this shit together. At the same time, my fingers wrap around my own serrated knife in my pocket, which I've unfurled with a quick *pop* of its spring. The dogs are at my feet, hackles up. My peripheral vision catches him rising to his feet with the blade in his hand.

We run.

My legs and arms move at rapid speed. I'm sprinting in boots and a winter coat and still we are flying. The dogs caught the fear—we are moving without thinking, just three fast-beating hearts creating cold dust on a gravel trail. It doesn't occur to me to turn around. What's the point? If he catches me, he catches me. All I can do is try.

As we near the curve of the trail just before the pedestrian bridge, I jolt my head to the side, only to witness an empty panorama. The man is all the way back near a stand of pines just past the North Avenue Bridge. The distance plus time doesn't make sense. In mere seconds, we traveled over a thousand feet.

I think: we might be coyotes and that man is just a man.

The dogs and I slow to a jog as we cross the bridge because we can. I keep my eyes on the distant figure and his knife. He watches me. He knows I'm watching. I smile.

Once we're on the west side of the river, I hook the leashes back onto the dogs and walk north toward home. I fumble with the phone in my pocket, annoyed with my shaking hands. The 911 dispatcher asks me twice for the cross streets, seeming not to understand that there were no streets—just land and water. She doesn't ask for a description, even when I say, "chased me with a big knife," and hangs up. Later, I scan the police dispatch log online and notice that the officer was sent to the wrong side of the river an hour and a half after I made the call. The status is listed as "Unable to Locate Complainant." Yes, I say to my computer screen. Because what was I supposed to do—stick around?

I think I should call back and inquire. I think of the woman with the arthritic Great Dane. So, I dial the police once more and am told that they'll look into it. I don't check the call log a second time. This city has made me selfish. I don't want to know.

*Possibility 7*

The morning quiet hasn't dissipated; it hasn't exploded into afternoon noise.

The day is not spent on the couch wrapped under blankets with the television on and heat blasting from the furnace. The dogs don't curl up in their beds, noses tucked under tails, as if they know today is not a good day.

I don't open a beer, and then another. Don't nap or sit staring at a book I can't read. Don't call my husband or my parents, who would only worry.

No, I put on my boots and go back outside. This is what Milwaukee wants you to do, is the only thing you can do. Move forward, shoulders back, knife in pocket. *Pop, pop, pop.* The Rust Belt is sinking under its segregation, lost jobs, and broken promises. Look at its angry men. In our neighborhood, the Polish Flats—separated by two feet of weeds and grass on either side—are tacked over with vinyl siding to hide the rotting wood. Still, I don't think about the house in the quiet field somewhere on the coast.

Instead, I tell my neighbors that we will live in this place as animals. Ragged-coated coyotes still haunt the woods on either side of the river; I know this because my dogs smell them and start to pant, overwhelmed either by their desire to kill them or join them—I don't know. We will walk north against the currents, even though eventually everything flows into the wide mouth of Lake Michigan, into that massive blue body of water, as impressive as any ocean.

I swear to you, I've heard it: The sound of fear moves its hulking waves instead of moon tides. Listen to what I'm saying. Tell me it's not possible.

# Epilogue

*Where is it still quiet?*

As technology, transport and industry continue to encroach upon the last remaining quiet places, human-made noise pollutes almost every forest, mountain, and ocean on earth.

(It's a depressing subject but we should know the facts.)

In 2017, the U.S. Department of Transportation found that 97 percent of the country is subjected to noise from aviation and interstate highways. And another 2017 study from Colorado State University reported that human-made noise doubled environmental sound in 63 percent of U.S. protected areas, as well as produced a tenfold or greater increase in 21 percent of those protected areas.

This proliferation of noise does more than irk dog walkers like me. Research shows that noise pollution is contributing to changing wildlife patterns and the depletion of the populations of certain species. Birds and frogs are unable to hear mating calls and animals may abandon their territory due not only to an inability to hear, but to the physiological effects of noise. Like humans, animals experience increased heart rates, respiratory issues, lower birth weights, and overall stress from noise.

In some areas animals can't even hear approaching predators, nevertheless listen for and hunt down prey, find their way back to their homes, and navigate unfamiliar territory.

And this isn't just a land problem. In dark waters, sound is used as the primary sense for most animals. It serves as a tool for communication, navigation, hunting, mating, and overall survival. Now, noise pollution caused by underwater drilling for oil and gas, shipping traffic, military sonar, and other industrial sources torments aquatic wildlife.

Noise confuses the sonar of whales and dolphins, causing them to beach themselves on land in a desperate attempt to escape the noise.

Marine mammals are dying of cerebral hemorrhaging due to the intense reverberations. Fish populations have been heavily reduced in areas of higher noise pollution. And squid, cuttlefish, and octopi sustain noise-related damage to sensitive organs, causing them to lose their sense of perception and balance, thus killing them.

*OKAY, BUT AGAIN, where is it still quiet?*

One moment—I want to be clear: I'm not implying that the unnaturalness of noise pollution should deter people from making noise. My god, *be loud.* Sound can be motivating, endorphin producing, empowering, comforting, chilling, inspiring, and a reason to get out of bed. Music can tie people together, unite families and communities and countries.

It can represent a culture, an era, a movement or emotion . . .

It can be healing or calming or traumatic, but whatever it is, it's amazing.

The problem is the progress. The clamor. The money. We've gone too far and forgotten what is lost when we only seek to expand.

*THE QUIET . . . ?*

For starters, my family's home is quiet. The last time I heard from my sister was in August 2018, two days before my thirty-second birthday and about a year and a half before COVID-19 penetrated U.S. borders. Her email was brief. She lamented that she needed to break off all communication with me just as she had with my parents several months before. Her final words? *I love you.* Out of respect for her wishes, I haven't attempted contact.

Of course, I did write a book that's largely about her, so . . . like most memoirists, I earn zero points for secret-keeping. The silence was simply overwhelming. I didn't know whether I wanted to yell or whisper, but I had to disrupt it.

*I'm sorry.*

The pandemic brought more changes: by early 2020, our collective actions to contain the deadly coronavirus drastically reduced urban noise pollution. Journalists described formerly bustling places with terms like "eerie," "dead," "forlorn," and "ghost town." Yet, this sudden reduction of harmful noise pollution also allowed city residents a brief listen in on a preindustrial past in which we weren't inundated by a constant, stress-inducing cacophony.

While the halt of normal human activity is clearly not a sustainable way of lessening chronic unnatural noise, the experience of existing in a more natural space could serve a purpose. As we grieve and heal and return to public spaces, I hope we'll better heed the advice of public health officials, city planners, and environmentalists by enacting policies to reduce the decibels.

WHERE ELSE IS *it still quiet?*

When you go searching for natural sound, you will struggle to find it. As reported by the acoustic ecologist, Gordon Hempton, there are only a few vestiges left in the U.S. that are free from human-made noise. As of late 2019, these places include:

The Hoh Rainforest in Olympic National Park, Washington
Haleakala National Park in Hawaii
The Boundary Waters Canoe Area in Minnesota

In the effort to protect them from us, the noisemakers, Hempton doesn't wish to disclose any other unpolluted locations; already, with climate change, these soundscapes face overwhelming daily threats. Of course, noise pollution is relative—in the Hoh Rainforest, for example, it stems from a rare airplane flying high overhead—but the result of trapped greenhouse gas emissions will be far louder if we fail to reverse or stop the damage.

Have you ever heard the roar of a wildfire or flood?

So, like a lowly, trembling fox cornered against a stone wall, I suppose it's best to leave quiet alone if you discover it. Back out slow, your movements just a murmur. Protect it from further disruption. Or go home and yell about it to anyone who will listen—I don't know. Just remember, suffering has a sound. You too know its toll.

# Bibliography

Augoyard, Jean-François, and Henry Torgue, eds. *Sonic Experience: A Guide to Everyday Sounds*. Translated by Andra McCartney and David Paquette. Montreal: McGill-Queen's University Press, 2005.

Barratt, Emma L., and Nick J. Davis. "Autonomous Sensory Meridian Response (ASMR): A Flow-like Mental State." *PeerJ* 3 (March 26, 2015): e851, https://doi.org/10.7717/peerj.851.

Bethea, Brittaney Jewel. "Effects of Segregation Negatively Impact Health." *The Source*, Washington University in St. Louis, January 25, 2016, https://source.wustl.edu/2013/11/effects-of-segregation-negatively-impact-health/.

Beutel, Manfred E., Claus Jünger, Eva M. Klein, Philipp Wild, Karl Lackner, Maria Blettner, Harald Binder et al. "Noise Annoyance Is Associated with Depression and Anxiety in the General Population—the Contribution of Aircraft Noise." *PLOS ONE* 11, no. 5 (2016): e0155357, https://doi.org/10.1371/journal.pone.0155357.

Buffenstein, Alyssa. "12 Sound Artists Changing Your Perception of Art." *Artnet*, August 4, 2016, https://news.artnet.com/art-world/12-sound-artists-changing-perception-art-587054.

Bureau of Transportation Statistics. "Under a Quarter of Population Exposed to Office-Type Transportation Noise." November 18, 2020, https://www.bts.gov/newsroom/national-transportation-noise-map.

Buxton, Rachel T., Megan F. McKenna, Daniel Mennitt, Emma Brown, Kurt Fristrup, Kevin R. Crooks, Lisa M. Angeloni, et al. "Anthropogenic Noise in US National Parks—Sources and Spatial Extent." *Frontiers in Ecology and the Environment* 17, no. 10 (December 2019): 559–64, https://doi.org/10.1002/fee.2112.

Casey, Evan. "ShotSpotter Program Receives State Grant." *Shepherd Express*, October 25, 2018, www.shepherdexpress.com/news/daily-dose/shotspotter-program-receives-state-grant/#/questions/.

Casey, Joan A. "Urban Noise Pollution Is Worst in Poor and Minority Neighborhoods and Segregated Cities." *PBS*, October 7, 2017, https://www.pbs.org/newshour/nation/urban-noise-pollution-worst-poor-minority-neighborhoods-segregated-cities.

Casey, Joan A., Rachel Morello-Frosch, Daniel J. Mennitt, Kurt Fristrup, Elizabeth L. Ogburn, and Peter James. "Race/Ethnicity, Socioeconomic Status, Residential Segregation, and Spatial Variation in Noise Exposure in the Contiguous United States." National Institute of Environmental Health Sciences, U.S. Department of Health and Human Services, July 25, 2017, https://ehp.niehs.nih.gov/doi/10.1289/ehp898.

Centers for Disease Control and Prevention. "What Noises Cause Hearing Loss?" Last reviewed October 7, 2019, https://www.cdc.gov/nceh/hearing_loss/what_noises_cause_hearing_loss.html.

Center for the Treatment and Study of Anxiety, Perelman School of Medicine, University of Pennsylvania. "Post-Traumatic Stress Disorder," accessed September 15, 2019, https://www.med.upenn.edu/ctsa/ptsd_symptoms.html.

Chanda, Mona Lisa, and Daniel J. Levitin. "The Neurochemistry of Music." *Trends in Cognitive Sciences* 17, no. 4 (2013): 179–93, https://doi.org/10.1016/j.tics.2013.02.007.

Chepesiuk, Ron. "Decibel Hell: The Effects of Living in a Noisy World." *Environmental Health Perspectives* 113, no. 1 (January 2005): A34–41, https://doi.org/10.1289/ehp.113-a34.

Chion, Michel. *Sound: An Acoulogical Treatise*. Translated by James A. Steintrager. Durham NC: Duke University Press, 2016.

Clifford, Georgina, Tim Dalgleish, and Caitlin Hitchcock. "Prevalence of Auditory Pseudohallucinations in Adult Survivors of Physical and Sexual Trauma with Chronic Post-Traumatic Stress Disorder (PTSD)." *Behaviour Research and Therapy* 111 (December 2018): 113–18, https://doi.org/10.1016/j.brat.2018.10.015.

Cornman, Dave. "Effects of Noise on Wildlife." Nature Sounds Society, accessed November 5, 2020, http://www.naturesounds.org/conservenw.html.

Dahl, Melissa. "'Whisper Porn' Has Apparently Stopped Working for Some People." *The Cut*, September 26, 2016, https://www.thecut.com/2016/09/asmr-immunity-is-apparently-a-real-thing.html.

Daley, Jason. "Flowers Sweeten up When They Sense Bees Buzzing." *Smithsonian Magazine*, January 18, 2019, www.smithsonianmag.com/smart-news/flowers-sweeten-when-they-hear-bees-buzzing-180971300/.

Davila, Vianna. "S. A. Cuts Funding to $550K Gunshot Detection Program That Resulted in 4 Arrests." *San Antonio Express-News*, August 15, 2017, www.mysanantonio.com/news/local/article/City-pulls-plug-on-pricey-gunshot-detection-system-11817475.php.

Drange, Matt. "ShotSpotter Alerts Police to Lots of Gunfire, But Produces Few Tangible Results." *Forbes*, July 24, 2017, www.forbes.com/sites/mattdrange/2016/11/17/shotspotter-alerts-police-to-lots-of-gunfire-but-produces-few-tangible-results/#20bddf55229e.

Etchells, Pete. "ASMR and 'Head Orgasms': What's the Science behind It?" *Guardian*, January 8, 2016, https://www.theguardian.com/science/head-quarters/2016/jan/08/asmr-and-head-orgasms-whats-the-science-behind-it.

European Environment Agency. "Environmental Noise." Last modified November 26, 2019, https://www.eea.europa.eu/airs/2018/environment-and-health/environmental-noise.

Fernyhough, Charles. "Do Deaf People Hear an Inner Voice?" *Psychology Today*, January 24, 2014, https://www.psychologytoday.com/us/blog/the-voices-within/201401/do-deaf-people-hear-inner-voice.

Fetterman, Mindy. "Seeking a Quiet Place in a Nation of Noise." *Stateline*, The Pew Charitable Trusts, April 16, 2018, https://www.pewtrusts.org/en/research-and-analysis/blogs/stateline/2018/04/16/seeking-a-quiet-place-in-a-nation-of-noise.

Fink, Daniel. Letter to the editor. *New York Times*, July 23, 2017, https://www.nytimes.com/2017/07/23/opinion/noise-is-a-health-hazard.html.

Fink, Daniel J. "What Is a Safe Noise Level for the Public?" *American Journal of Public Health* 107, no. 1 (January 2017): 44–45, https://doi.org/10.2105/AJPH.2016.303527.

Foley, Dennis. "What Is Flutter Echo and How Does It Apply to Room Acoustics?" Acoustic Fields, last modified November 3, 2019, https://www.acousticfields.com/flutter-echo-apply-room-acoustics/.

Fountain, Henry. "It's Still Dark Out, So Why Are the Birds Singing Away?" *New York Times*, May 8, 2007, https://www.nytimes.com/2007/05/08/science/08observ.html.

Fuller, Richard A., Philip H. Warren, and Kevin J. Gaston. "Daytime Noise Predicts Nocturnal Singing in Urban Robins." *Biology Letters* 3, no. 4 (August 2007): 368–70, https://doi.org/10.1098/rsbl.2007.0134.

Goldsby, Tamara L., Michael E. Goldsby, Mary McWalters, and Paul J. Mills. "Effects of Singing Bowl Sound Meditation on Mood, Tension, and Well-Being: An Observational Study." *Journal of Evidence-Based Complementary & Alternative Medicine* 22, no. 3 (July 2017): 401–6, https://doi.org/10.1177/2156587216668109.

Gubar, Susan. "When Music Is the Best Medicine." *New York Times*, September 26, 2019, https://www.nytimes.com/2019/09/26/well/live/music-therapy-cancer.html.

Heller, Morris F., and Moe Bergman. "Tinnitus Aurium in Normally Hearing Persons." *Annals of Otology, Rhinology & Laryngology* 62, no. 1 (1953): 73–83, https://doi.org/10.1177/000348945306200107.

Hempton, Gordon. "Silence and the Presence of Everything." On Being Project, August 29, 2019, https://onbeing.org/programs/gordon-hempton-silence-and-the-presence-of-everything/.

Hu, Winnie. "New York Is a Noisy City. One Man Got Revenge." *New York Times*, June 4, 2019, https://www.nytimes.com/2019/06/04/nyregion/nyc-loud-noisy.html.

Jones, Nicola. "Ocean Uproar: Saving Marine Life from a Barrage of Noise." *Nature*, April 10, 2019, https://www.nature.com/articles/d41586-019-01098-6.

Jongseok, Lim, Kukju Kweon, Hyo-Won Kim, Seung Woo Cho, Jangho Park, and Chang Sun Sim. "Negative Impact of Noise and Noise Sensitivity on Mental Health in Childhood." *Noise & Health* 20, no. 96 (September–October 2018): 199–211, https://www.ncbi.nlm.nih.gov/pmc/articles/pmc6301087/.

Kagge, Erling. *Silence: In the Age of Noise.* Translated by Becky L. Crook. New York: Vintage, 2018.

Kakutani, Michiko. "Power to Soothe the Savage Breast and Animate the Hemispheres." *New York Times*, November 20, 2007, https://www.nytimes.com/2007/11/20/books/20kaku.html.

Kapchan, Deborah. "Body." In *Keywords in Sound*, edited by David Novak and Matt Sakakeeny, 33–44. Durham NC: Duke University Press, 2015.

Keizer, Garret. *The Unwanted Sound of Everything We Want: A Book about Noise*. New York: PublicAffairs, 2012.

Kelly, Caleb, ed. *Sound*. Whitechapel: *Documents of Contemporary Art*. Cambridge MA: MIT Press, 2011.

Knight, Will. "Urban Nightingales' Songs Are Illegally Loud." *New Scientist*, May 5, 2004, https://www.newscientist.com/article/dn4964-urban-nightingales-songs-are-illegally-loud/.

Kolomatsky, Michael. "The Noisiest Places in New York." *New York Times*, August 2, 2018, https://www.nytimes.com/2018/08/02/realestate/the-noisiest-places-in-new-york.html.

Loewy, Joanne, Kristen Stewart, Ann-Marie Dassler, Aimee Telsey, and Peter Homel. "The Effects of Music Therapy on Vital Signs, Feeding, and Sleep in Premature Infants." *Pediatrics* 131, no. 5 (May 2013): 902–18, https://doi.org/10.1542/peds.2012-1367.

Mays, Jeffery C. "Why Construction Noise Is Keeping You Up at 3 A.M." *New York Times*, September 27, 2019, https://www.nytimes.com/2019/09/27/nyregion/noise-construction-sleep-nyc.html.

Museum of Endangered Sounds, March 20, 2020, http://savethesounds.info/.

Novak, David, and Matt Sakakeeny, eds. *Keywords in Sound*. Durham NC: Duke University Press, 2015.

NYU Langone Medical Center, New York University Grossman School of Medicine. "How Exposure to Brief Trauma and Sudden Sounds Form Lasting Memories." *Science Daily*, August 24, 2015, https://www.sciencedaily.com/releases/2015/08/150824114553.htm.

Ouellette, Jennifer. "A Shot in the Dark: The Acoustics of Gunfire." *Scientific American*, November 9, 2011, Cocktail Party Physics, https://blogs.scientificamerican.com/cocktail-party-physics/a-shot-in-the-dark-the-acoustics-of-gunfire/.

Petitto, Laura Ann, Robert J. Zatorre, Kristine Gauna, E. J. Nikelski, Deanna Dostie, and Alan C. Evans. "Speech-like Cerebral Activity in Profoundly Deaf People Processing Signed Languages: Implications for the Neural Basis of Human Language." *PNAS* 97, no. 25 (December 2000): 13961–66, https://doi.org/10.1073/pnas.97.25.13961.

Poerio, Giulia Lara, Emma Blakey, Thomas J. Hostler, and Theresa Veltri. "More than a Feeling: Autonomous Sensory Meridian Response (ASMR)

Is Characterized by Reliable Changes in Affect and Physiology." *PLOS ONE* 13, no. 6 (2018): e0196645, https://doi.org/10.1371/journal.pone .0196645.

Randle, Aaron. "Building Is Booming 24/7. So Is the Noise." *New York Times*, September 27, 2019, https://www.nytimes.com/2019/09/27/nyregion /nyc-construction-noise.html.

Robbins, Jim. "Oceans Are Getting Louder, Posing Potential Threats to Marine Life." *New York Times*, January 22, 2019, https://www.nytimes .com/2019/01/22/science/oceans-whales-noise-offshore-drilling.html.

Sanchez, Bianca. "Gunshots or Fireworks? How to Tell the Difference." *Chicago Tribune*, July 3, 2019, https://www.chicagotribune .com/lifestyles/ct-life-gunshot-firework-tt-07032019-20190703 -llyatklb7vfujjvu45m5mhzoey-story.html.

Schafer, R. Murray. *The Soundscape: Our Sonic Environment and the Tuning of the World*. Rochester VT: Destiny Books, 1993.

Schmidt, Gary D., and Susan M. Felch, eds. *Winter: A Spiritual Biography of the Season*. Nashville TN: SkyLight Paths Publishing, 2003.

Sharma, Hari. "Meditation: Process and Effects." *Ayu* 36, no. 3 (July–September 2015): 233–37, https://doi.org/10.4103/0974-8520.182756.

Stanborough, Rebecca Joy. "The Uses and Benefits of Music Therapy." *Healthline*, last modified November 24, 2020, https://www.healthline .com/health/sound-healing.

Sterne, Jonathan. "Hearing." In *Keywords in Sound*, edited by David Novak and Matt Sakakeeny, 65–77. Durham NC: Duke University Press, 2015.

Stewart, Michael. "Recreational Firearm Noise Exposure." American Speech-Language-Hearing Association, accessed November 1, 2020, https://www .asha.org/public/hearing/Recreational-Firearm-Noise-Exposure/.

Surico, John. "My Quixotic Quest for Quiet in New York City." *Bloomberg*, June 21, 2019, CityLab, https://www.citylab.com/life/2019/06/noise -pollution-public-health-nyc-hush-city-data-maps/592225/.

Swinbourne, Charlie. "Noises in the Deaf of Night." *BBC News*, October 26, 2008, http://www.bbc.co.uk/ouch/features/noises-in-the-deaf-of-night .shtml.

"Train, Road Traffic Biggest Sources of Noise Pollution in Mumbai: NEERI Study." *Hindustan Times*, August 14, 2018, https://www.hindustantimes .com/mumbai-news/train-road-traffic-biggest-sources-of-noise-pollution -in-mumbai-neeri-study/story-Eieqmiu8pzrMilklhczhwp.html.

Voegelin, Salomé. *Listening to Noise and Silence: Towards a Philosophy of Sound Art*. New York: Continuum, 2010.

Wagner, Kate. "City Noise Might Be Making You Sick." *Atlantic*, February 20, 2018, https://www.theatlantic.com/technology/archive/2018/02/city -noise-might-be-making-you-sick/553385/.

Zaraska, Marta. "Can Plants Hear?" *Scientific American*, May 17, 2017, Biology, www.scientificamerican.com/article/can-plants-hear/.

## Acknowledgments

I wrote this book over several years, then rewrote this book, then revised it again and again and again. I edited my work obsessively—again, over years of time—and looked for an agent, then a publisher, and waited, waited, waited. So, what I'm saying is, like so many books, it's remarkable that this one exists at all, and that I still exist with it. But for this book's physical presence in this world, I have many wonderful people to thank.

Whenever I threatened to throw my laptop in the trash, my husband, Kumar, gave me a calm and sympathetic look before saying, "We both know that's never going to happen." Of course, he was right. Kumar, thank you so much for being my partner through what's felt like an endless test of endurance. No matter what happens, I will remember my life as a good one—an extremely fortunate one—because I had you in it. *Thank you.*

Thank you, as well, to my sister. I'm unsure if you'll read this book, or even realize that it was published, but you were my constant in a messy, often unkind world, and I'm forever grateful. I hope you are enjoying the happiest, most joyous, of lives.

Thank you to my parents for your decades of generosity, support, and immense sacrifices.

Thank you to my parents-in-law, who I know would do anything for us, and to Jayanta, for all the laughs and long talks.

Thank you to all the rescue dogs in my life, who've walked with me through many tough times.

And thank you to my beloved Ramy for making me sing again. I still can't believe that you're here. I still can't believe that I deserve you.

Thank you, as well, to my agent, Jennifer Thompson, for your incredible persistence and wisdom. Furthermore, thank to my project editor, Abigail Kwambamba, acquiring editor, Courtney Ochsner, and copyeditor, Anne McPeak, for your tireless efforts in readying this book for publication.

Who else? Thank you to my dear friends and fellow writers, including Jennifer Crystal, Emily Avery-Miller, Lauren Sieben Sternecky, Abby Travis, Lauren Kay Johnson, Shannon DeScioli, Martin Hansen, Ashley Wells, Caitlin McGill, Laura Tetreault, Miranda Dynan, Susannah Clark Matt, Krysta Voskowsky, John Fantin, Sati Mookherjee, Theresa Fisher, John DeVore, Jyni Ekins, Emily Maloney, Su Cho, and Angela Voras-Hills.

For your incredible camaraderie, thank you to Katrien Mattis, Anshika Verma, Mariah Mateo Sarpong, Kwaku Sarpong, Yolande Grobler, Dan Hogan, Teresa O'Day, Kandice Kardell, Kate Ward, and Matt Filipowicz.

Lastly, there are several people who provided mentorship and encouragement along the way. Thank you to Richard Hoffman (I wouldn't have made it this far without you), Jerald Walker, Joan Wickersham, Megan Marshall, Natalie Dykstra, Doug Whynott, Jane Brox, and my third-grade teacher, Mrs. Trolliet. I also must extend my gratitude to Emerson College, the Virginia Center for the Creative Arts, and Bread Loaf, as well as *Cream City Review, Seneca Review, Indiana Review, North American Review,* and Belt Publishing's City Anthology Series, which published portions of this book.

My life could have taken such a different, darker direction if it weren't for all the support I've received, so thank you all for reading. Thank you all so much for listening.

"The Sound of a Poet," originally published as "A List of Sounds That Can Be Heard in Milwaukee," in *The Milwaukee Anthology*, ed. Justin Kern (Cleveland OH: Belt Publishing, 2019).

"The Sound of Nothing," *Indiana Review* 41, no. 1 (Summer 2019).

"The Sound of an Imitated Ocean," *Cream City Review* 43, no. 1 (Spring/Summer 2019).

"The Sound of Undoing," *North American Review* 304, no. 1 (Winter 2019).

"The Sound of a Whisper," originally published as "Before Going Quiet," *Seneca Review* 51, no. 2 (Fall 2021).

## IN THE AMERICAN LIVES SERIES

*The Twenty-Seventh Letter of
the Alphabet: A Memoir*
by Kim Adrian

*Fault Line*
by Laurie Alberts

*Pieces from Life's Crazy Quilt*
by Marvin V. Arnett

*Songs from the Black Chair:
A Memoir of Mental Illness*
by Charles Barber

*This Is Not the Ivy
League: A Memoir*
by Mary Clearman Blew

*Body Geographic*
by Barrie Jean Borich

*Driving with Dvořák: Essays
on Memory and Identity*
by Fleda Brown

*Searching for Tamsen Donner*
by Gabrielle Burton

*Island of Bones: Essays*
by Joy Castro

*American Lives: A Reader*
edited by Alicia Christensen
introduced by Tobias Wolff

*If This Were Fiction: A
Love Story in Essays*
by Jill Christman

*Get Me Through Tomorrow:
A Sister's Memoir of Brain
Injury and Revival*
by Mojie Crigler

*Should I Still Wish: A Memoir*
by John W. Evans

*Out of Joint: A Private and
Public Story of Arthritis*
by Mary Felstiner

*Descanso for My Father:
Fragments of a Life*
by Harrison Candelaria Fletcher

*My Wife Wants You to Know
I'm Happily Married*
by Joey Franklin

*Weeds: A Farm Daughter's Lament*
by Evelyn I. Funda

*Falling Room*
by Eli Hastings

*Borderline Citizen: Dispatches
from the Outskirts of Nationhood*
by Robin Hemley

*The Distance Between: A Memoir*
by Timothy J. Hillegonds

*Opa Nobody*
by Sonya Huber

*Pain Woman Takes Your Keys, and Other Essays from a Nervous System*
by Sonya Huber

*Hannah and the Mountain: Notes toward a Wilderness Fatherhood*
by Jonathan Johnson

*Under My Bed and Other Essays*
by Jody Keisner

*Local Wonders: Seasons in the Bohemian Alps*
by Ted Kooser

*A Certain Loneliness: A Memoir*
by Sandra Gail Lambert

*Bigger than Life: A Murder, a Memoir*
by Dinah Lenney

*What Becomes You*
by Aaron Raz Link and Hilda Raz

*Queen of the Fall: A Memoir of Girls and Goddesses*
by Sonja Livingston

*The Virgin of Prince Street: Expeditions into Devotion*
by Sonja Livingston

*Anything Will Be Easy after This: A Western Identity Crisis*
by Bethany Maile

*Such a Life*
by Lee Martin

*Turning Bones*
by Lee Martin

*In Rooms of Memory: Essays*
by Hilary Masters

*Island in the City: A Memoir*
by Micah McCrary

*Between Panic and Desire*
by Dinty W. Moore

*To Hell with It: Of Sin and Sex, Chicken Wings, and Dante's Entirely Ridiculous, Needlessly Guilt-Inducing "Inferno"*
by Dinty W. Moore

*Let Me Count the Ways: A Memoir*
by Tomás Q. Morín

*Shadow Migration: Mapping a Life*
by Suzanne Ohlmann

*Meander Belt: Family, Loss, and Coming of Age in the Working-Class South*
by M. Randal O'Wain

*Sleep in Me*
by Jon Pineda

*The Solace of Stones: Finding a Way through Wilderness*
by Julie Riddle

*Works Cited: An Alphabetical Odyssey of Mayhem and Misbehavior*
by Brandon R. Schrand

To order or obtain more
information on these or other
University of Nebraska Press
titles, visit nebraskapress.unl.edu.